GRA...
CR
WAS
FUN

by

W.E. Downes

Castle of Dreams Books

First impression

Published by

Castle of Dreams Books
8 Pease Street
Darlington
DL1 4EU
UK

☎/🖷 01325 381466

dreamer@dial.pipex.com

Published from camera-ready artwork (sic)

ISBN 1 86185 222 3

DEDICATED
To the memory of

Ernie Bishop, Roy Buck, Bill Davies,
George and Ken Reece, Ben Roberts,
Henry Seedhouse, Marcus Thomas
And Tommy Williamson

ACKNOWLEDGEMENTS

To my wife Lily for her encouragement to put on paper stories she has
heard many times before

To Michael Vockins for writing a foreword that endorses the spirit of the
book that all cricket should be fun

To Michael Graham without who's help and advice the book would never
have got into print

To Pauline Boyce Lewis who very kindly supplied most of the
illustrations

FOREWORD

Readers of Eddie Downes' warm and colourful reminiscences may not all know Marcus Thomas, or George Reece, Eric Heath or Tommy Williamson – but their counterparts will be known in every club in England. We will know their likenesses in our own clubs.

We may not have encountered umpire Herman Higgins, but we have all encountered the umpire with eccentricities who sits on a shooting stick [an expression which recalls Brian Johnston's spoonerism as he described the batting stance of Henry Horton, the prolific Hampshire run maker], smokes furtively at square leg, whose rate of decision making increases with great rapidity as the opening time of the local hostelry approaches, or who seems ever anxious to find the moment to implement one of the more obscure laws of cricket to the bafflement of all.

We may not even know the village of Worfield or its cricket club but, assuredly, we shall know many like them.

We know, too, the stalwart players and supporters of every such club, the folk who are the life blood of our national game. Not all will be oozing with talent, and their will be those who loyally turn out week by week, in drizzle and in harvest sun, whether they get to bat or bowl or achieve success or endure failure, simply because the game had taken a hold on them and courses through their veins.

These are the folk who play, and take their turn at preparing the ground, cleaning kit, sweeping pavilions, umpiring, scoring, putting up the numbers on the scoreboards, making teas, serving drinks, fundraising – all those things which every dedicated cricketer [and his wife or girlfriend] has shared in.

We know too of the never ending dressing room selection of teams [for England, the village, the world, the uglies, and whole hosts more], of the debates [seldom conclusive] on what is important for the game or what compares favourably [or unfavourably] with cricket "in my day". We have all been challenged by the testing quiz questions. If we have not visited "The Dog" or "Davenport Arms" we have all enjoyed the hospitality of their local equivalents. We have all expressed our affectionate regard of our own cricketing heroes.

Here then interwoven in Eddie Downes' reminiscences – ranging from the respectful to the wry! – are splendid reminders of our own cricket and of all that serves, and has served, our game for so long and so well. Here are reminders of a wonderful game full of characters, of the variety of venues in which it is played, the stalwarts who play it. Above all here we are reminded of the great traditions of the game, the richness of its customs and – more than anything – the great affection that cricket engenders amongst us all, and for which we are enduringly grateful.

Read on, reminisce, relish – and give thanks for a great game and a way of life it embraces.

The Rev'd Michael Vockins

CONTENTS

Foreword by The Rev Michael Vockins

INTRODUCTION

Cricket has been played for around 300 years and at Worfield in Shropshire for over 100 years. My story starts at Worfield just after the Second World War in 1946.

There have been countless books written about the game over the years by people like Cardus, Swanton, Arlott and the inspiration for this book, Brian Johnston, for it was dear old Johnners more than anyone that recognized that the game of cricket should be fun. Season after season, books are written or "ghosted" by international cricketers following tours or test match series. Many of them quite predictable in their content.

The computer has taken over and statistics are churned out by the mile. Very interesting, but also very boring unless you are an absolute fanatic. Many stories have been told and will continue to be told concerning characters in the first class game, but few from club cricket, the "grassroots" of the game.

This is an attempt to redress the situation. Like Johnners, I make no apology for including stories not the least bit related to cricket, provided they are humorous.

* * * * *

There is a Quiz of First Class Cricket Questions running through the book, answers to be found at the back.

The words of Neville Cardus describe the contents of this book best when he said, "To go to a cricket match for nothing but cricket is though a man were to go into an inn for nothing but drink".

Constructive criticism is offered with regard to the excessive number of no balls bowled and the slow over rate. Richie Benaud is taken to task over his attitude to the front foot rule. The dilemma facing umpires with the existing rather vague wide ball law is identified and a positive solution proposed.

Formats for impromptu cricket in the form of a single wicket competition, an intense six-a-side tournament are included together with rules for indoor cricket, not forgetting that cricket has a social side. There are also observations on the Tour Party Selections and a basic Blueprint for the future.

If a ball when bowled is called a wide, should it be deemed as having-been received by the batsman? Read what the experts say.

Thoughts on the World Cup and proposals for future tournaments are expressed.

* * * * *

There are other items to test your Cricket knowledge and observation skills, answers at the back.

THAT'S CRICKET

It's the end of the day
and close of play
handshakes all round
as we leave the ground.

There was the odd duck
for those out of luck.
A five wicket haul
with the new ball.

For others, a hand
in a century stand.
But what won the match
was a sensational catch.

Old what's his name
last ball of the game.
Stuck out his mitt
to a really big hit.

In his hand it did fix
and saved a certain six
God bless his soul
he did not bat or bowl.

Nowt went his way
as he fielded all day.
It goes without saying
they'd forgot he was playing.

But that last move
just goes to prove
if you have heart
you can still play your part.

No matter how old
when catches you hold
in the deep or at the wicket
you can still be the hero at cricket.

IN THE LONG GRASS

Would you believe it is possible to carry on a love affair that has the approval of your wife and, on occasions, the encouragement to bring your sons and grandsons up to follow your example with the same degree of passion?

My love for the game of cricket began about 50 years ago and has not waned with the passing of the years.

As a school boy, I had been given "the stick" by Mr. Knowles, our much respected Headmaster. It was for breaking a window in one of the classrooms whilst playing football in a forbidden area. A week later, I was playing cricket in the school field when I hit the cricket ball right through the greenhouse roof. Later I hit another through a window of the newly erected school canteen. A pal of mine, Maurice Speke, broke another one and we both thought we would be in trouble, but, as we were playing cricket in the correct place, nothing was said. We both reckoned that it was a good game, this game called cricket.

The builders put a fence of wire netting up to protect the windows of the new building. Maurice promptly hit a ball that dropped neatly over the fence, crash, right through the kitchen window. The cook was not happy.

We were asked to pitch the stumps further up the field, the trouble was the river Worfe was in flood and we had to keep on wading in after the ball. We tried another spot, the beehives were the next to suffer, and the bees were almost as angry as the cook.

We finally settled on the most central position, we then operated on a most definitely six, out, and fetch it basis. The problem was we kept on playing in this one position and the pitch became bare and rock hard, it

FCCQ Question 1:
Mowing machines were used for the first time on cricket grounds about 1850. How was the job done before that?

was like playing on concrete. a tall dark lad named Neil Simes was bowling to me one lunch time when the ball got up off a length and hit me in the mouth knocking my top front teeth back into my mouth. I instinctively put my thumb behind them and strengthened them out, my lips were swollen and for about 3 days I was only able to drink through a straw.

Following this experience I would like to see artificial wickets laid on all school playing fields to encourage youngsters to play the game at every single opportunity.

Just after the war in 1946, Worfield cricket club started playing cricket again in Finchers field opposite the recreation room. As my mother said, "You used to haunt the flipping cricket ground."

Ernie Bishop and Henry Seedhouse were the captains in those days. "Bring your kit in case we are short" they used to say. "You can always score anyway." I didn't mind scoring, you had to concentrate and it was a good way to learn the game, but I really wanted to play.

When I did play, I got plenty of exercise, fielding at deep fine leg both ends. If Eric Heath was keeping wickets after a liquid lunch at the Wheel, I got plenty to do. Occasionally I got in to bat at no.11, often finishing 0 not out as the other batsman threw his wicket away. This did not diminish my enthusiasm for the game, and if there was any sign of cricket being played, be it a match or practice.

FCCQ Question 2:
In 1787, play began on Thomas Lord's first cricket ground
Where was this sited?

WORFIELD CRICKET TEAM AT OPENING OF NEW GROUND IN DAVENPORT PARK 1954

Back Row: Aubrey Glaze, Eddie Downes, Bill Davies, Denis Fincher, Marcus Thomas, Jeff Hughes
Front Row: George Reece, Ken Reece, Henry Seedhouse, Ben Roberts, Ernie Bishop

There was a concrete strip and matting laid with nets along side the small brick built telephone exchange. Bill Davis would come along saying "I've got a new bat I want to try out." When it was just the young lads bowling at him, he would place a sixpence on the top of each stump saying "You can have any that you knock off." I took half a crown off him one night, after that, he only used to place a coin on the middle stump. At least the practice used to do him some good. I saw him score a brilliant 97 at Boulton & Paul's just failing to be the club's first century maker.

It was a different ball game in those days. Before a game, the first job was to remove the barbed wire fencing from around the well-maintained square. The outfield was grazed by cattle and a pair of carthorses. If the cattle had not been on the field for a day or two, the grass on the outfield would be long with the odd dried pancake of cow dung. If, however, the cattle had been in the field that morning, or were still in the field albeit not in the playing area, the grass would be shorter but there would be a lot more pancakes of cow dung and the majority of them would be soft. The older players fielded round the bat on the square, but the young 'uns were sent out into the deep.

Into the deep had different connotations then when you consider the length of the grass. Now, there were many things you had to think about in the short time you had to field the ball. If you were lucky the ball would stop quickly in a thick clump of grass and you would just have to pick it up and throw it in and restrict the batsman to a single. Well fielded.

If, however, it landed on a hard baked pancake, it would shoot off at great pace, often changing direction, making you look a fool as if you were running round in circles.

FCCQ Question 3:
Lord's second ground opened at North Bank in 1809, but was later bisected by the construction of what?

Now, if it landed in a soft pancake of cow dung there was a lot to consider. Did you kick it about a bit too clean it in the long grass, or did you ignore the fact that it was coated with a sticky strong smelling substance and throw it in as quickly as possible? Whether this was before or after tea might influence your decision. If you did pick it up, who was keeping wickets and who was the bowler? If Eric Heath was behind the stumps, he wouldn't catch it cleanly anyway [Oh dear, that's a terrible pun]. Perhaps the sticky coating might help him hold onto it for once. If, however, it was the immaculate Brian Johnson [no, not Johnners] you could not expect him to attempt to catch it, so it would be allowed to pass through as an overthrow to be cleaned by the long grass on the other side of the square, thus passing your dilemma onto the fielder on the other side of the wickets. As regard to the bowlers, the same attitude would apply to Freddy Cox as Brian Johnson, as he most likely needed his kit for a game in the RAF the next day. Now, if it was Tommy Williamson, being a farm worker, he wouldn't let a bit of cow muck bother him and he wouldn't like the idea of overthrows coming off his bowling either. As I stated, there was a lot to think about, yet there was plenty of conflicting advice.

Brian Johnston of Test Match Special fame has included a version of this particular story I am about to relate in one of his books, but I am able to give the authentic version because, as Max Boyce says "And I know because I was there."
Worfield Cricket Club were playing the Express and Star.

FCCQ Question 4:
Thomas Lord's third ground, on the present site, was opened and the turf transferred for the second time. In which year?

Tommy Williamson was bowling for Worfield and had just bowled the opening batsman. John Swallow, the visitors captain, came in and was promptly given out first ball L B W. He was hit on the front foot and obviously did not like the decision. As he was walking back to be pavilion a local wag called out " Never mind skipper, you will find you was out alright, have a look in the Express and Star tomorrow night." John Swallow, with the waxed ends of his black moustache twitching, snapped back "You look, I'm the editor."

Tommy Williamson was a very good opening bowler with a Brian Statham like accuracy. He had an extraordinary zigzag, stop-start type run up, but a fine delivery stride and follow through. One of his proudest moments was bowling Cyril Washbrook in an evening match on the Bridgnorth ground.

The present day over enthusiastic appealing by bowlers, such as demonstrated by Dominic Cork, was not Tommy's style. He would turn and in a softly spoken voice would say "How was that, umpire?" as if to say" He looked out to me, what do you think?" Believe it or not, it always seemed to be more effective than shouting.

Tommy used to bat down the order, but had the ability to occupy the crease, he used to take out his false teeth, wrap them in a handkerchief and put them in the back pocket of his flannels. He explained his reasons for doing this as follows. He said it stopped him turning his back on the ball in case he got hit in the teeth, and if he got hit in the mouth, his teeth would not be broken.

Tommy was one of the many local cricketers that I enjoyed

FCCQ Question 5.
He was either known as Dr. Grace or, better still, W. G. What first names did the initials W. G. stand for?

playing with over the years, and I feel the idiosyncrasies of such "grass roots" cricketers such as Tommy, should be recognized alongside those of household name test cricketers.

As a schoolboy, when I got to the ground, I used to count the players. I would get to 9 or 10 and then look for Em Cooper. Em was always last to arrive, already changed into his whites, except for his cricket boots that were tied together and slung over the handle bars of his push bike. I remember Em as a very static player, he was not a bad bat, but if the ball didn't go to the boundary, he rarely scored more than one run and a second run was definitely out of the question if the other batsman had hit it. He used to stand at point, and I mean stand. If the ball went past him he would always let someone else chase after it, but if it was catchable the ball would disappear into his enormous paddle like hands.

The pavilion consisted of one room where both teams changed together, so there was no space for an L B W sulking corner. Teas were taken across at the recreation room and were taken at 5.00pm sharp. There was no point in captains thinking they would have it between innings and bat on a bit longer and save time in having to go out again after tea which was frowned upon by the opposition. No, unless you enjoyed a cold cup of tea, tea was at 5.00pm because that was the time Mrs. Harley started pouring the tea and, as a mother of the pre-war cricketers, she was one of the old school and time was time.

FCCQ Question 6:
The W. G. Grace memorial gates were erected in St. John 's Wood Road, designed by architect Sir Herbert Baker in 1923. What did the same architect present in 1926?

Get it while it's hot Lads

It was Mrs. Harley, who was well over 80 years of age, who was given a box of groceries one Christmas by her neighbour. This included a box of tea-bags. Mrs. Harley was very pleased with the groceries and thanked her neighbour "It was very good of you to collect the tea samples, but it took me ages to cut the little bags open and empty the tea into the caddy".

The players had various occupations, and old Bish worked for Worfield Gardens who had just won a gold medal at the Chelsea flower show. The following Sunday, Bish was looking for his box as he was due to go out to bat. He turned his bag inside out and was still looking for it when two other players came in and asked "Have you seen that prize winning exhibit in the new hanging basket on the pavilion, very nice."
Need I say more.

FCCQ Question 7:
What year was the heavy roller first used at Lord's?

A family named Fincher farmed the land, hence the name "Fincher's Field". One of the sons, Denis, played and has the proud record of being the only player to have hit the ball over the river Worfe that runs alongside the field at the bottom of a slope behind where the pavilion was situated. A distance in excess of 120 yards. We will have to measure it one day.

There is no truth in the rumour that Denis trained their white horse to act as a sight-screen while he was batting and their black bull while he was bowling. It just happened that way.

As much as cricket was enjoyed on this ground, it was time to look for a more permanent base, and the players of today have these old stalwarts to thank for the foresight in providing the basis for the amenities enjoyed today.

Who's turn is it to move the sight screens?

FCCQ Question 8:
The only time any batsman has hit the ball over the pavilion at Lord's was in 1899, an Australian, MA Noble, was bowling. Who was the batsman?

AN ODE TO THE MEN O' THE WORFE

Through the endeavours of our leaders,
we found some land where we could play
The value of their thinking and hard
labours are there to see today

The site had been used before
as a camp for German prisoners of war
Worth bearing that in mind
as cricket is war of a different kind

When we proved to the owners
that our intentions were good and
sound An agreement was reached
that we could create a cricket ground

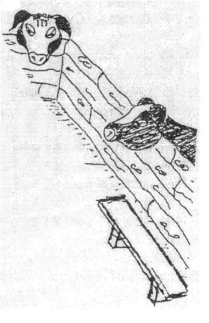

We had a ground, somewhere to play
but before the play could start there
was much to be done with the head
and with good heart

We set to work and fenced it off to
keep the cows away Then a few
seats were placed around and critics
had their say

East to west or north to south the
decision to be made which way
would the wickets run when the
square was laid

A Captive audience

All agreed that batting in the
evening sunshine can be fun
but not when facing a demon bowler running in out of the sun

It was ploughed and leveled in the
rain and in the sun raked and rolled
and we picked stone by the ton

Yes, we picked stone after stone by
the ton but, would you believe me
when I say "picking stone was fun"

A ton of fun!

To site the pavilion was
the next thing we had to do
to pick a spot with handy access
and an outstanding view

With an open field it is not
quite as simple to behold
to think it through and get it right
before a ball is bowled

Long term planning was the main
thought here to watch matches in the
future but with a pint of beer

To see it now with glass in hand gives
me cause to smile
Sons and grandsons playing and
that makes it all worthwhile

That's my boy!

PUTTING DOWN GRASS ROOTS

The first match on the present ground at Davenport Park, Worfield was played, quite rightly, against the old enemy – Claverly Cricket Club.

It will be seen from the photograph of the Worfield side that played on that day that I was the youngest player there. Sadly, there are only four of us left. However, I would like to recall some of the happy memories, which I am sure they would have enjoyed.

It will be seen from the photograph of the ground taken that day, shown on the cover, that a marquee was erected in which teas were served. However, for the remainder of that, and the next two seasons, we used to go and have tea in the basement of Davenport Hall. We used to all sit round a suitably covered full size snooker table.

I recall one day Bill Davies was at one end of the table and Henry Seedhouse at the other. "Pass the sugar down, please" said Bill. "How many lumps do you want?" asked Henry. "Three". "There you are" and tossed three lumps, one after the other, the length of the table – plop! plop! plop! right into Bill's cup of tea. As no one could top that, the sugar bowl was passed round hand to hand by other members.

FCCQ Question 9:
The first test match between England and Australia in England was played in 1880. Name the winning side and the margin.

21

Henry was the village Blacksmith and also a Farrier. There are grounds around Shropshire where Henry has left his trademark. He was never short of somewhere to hang his clothes, taking a horseshoe nail out of his pocket and, with the heel of his cricket boot Bang, Bang, Bang - problem solved.

Have you got a spare peg for me, Henry?

We were granted permission to use part of the Davenport Coat of Arms as our Club Badge with the motto *"Audentes Fortuna Juvat"* (Fortune favours the Brave) or more freely interpreted, God Bless the tailenders!

There was a period when the team had Club Blazers complete with the aforementioned badges.

FCCQ Question 10:
What unique record does John Hampshire hold?

One day, Sir Oliver Lease, who was the president of Warwickshire County Cricket Club, invited Henry, Bish, Ben and Marcus as his guests for a Test Match at Edgbaston. Just before the game was due to start, Sir Oliver said to Bernard Flack, the Groundsman, "Bernard, take Henry and the lads out to have a look at the wicket." "Very good, Sir" said Bernard. The television cameras had just tuned in and Brian Johnston was commentating

"Ah, here comes Bernard Flack and um, and um..." The cameras were quickly focussed on the clock and Brian Johnston resumed commentary saying "The umpires will be out in a minute" and, much to his relief "Here they are" just as Bernard and his party walked off the other side.

Bernard Flack became a very good friend to Worfield Cricket Club and came to our Annual Dinner for over 25 years. He was very helpful to us in those early years in laying the square, then one day said "You don't need me anymore, in fact, you had better come and have a look at Edgbaston for me, Marcus!"

Sir Oliver Lease was also president of M.C.C. and Shropshire County Cricket Club and a great enthusiast of the game.

There were a number of matches when Sir Oliver's eleven played against selected opposition such as New Zealand House or Australia House, depending on the touring team at the time.

I remember playing in a game for Sir Oliver with Henry, Ben and Marcus from our Club, Tom Pritchard and Ray Hitchcock from Warwickshire, a fellow named Barr from Scotland and a Guards Officer named Towers was wicket keeper – he was

absolutely immaculate with white silk cravat and all! When we went out to field, Tom Pritchard opened the bowling and this Major Towers asked who he was. "He's Warwickshire's opening bowler" (and, according to

---

FCCQ Question 11:
In Ashes Test Matches, how many record wicket partnerships for Australia does D. G. Bradman feature in?

Wisden, as fast as any in the country at that time). "Oh, I'd better stand back," said the keeper.

After the first ball he went up behind the stumps to take the second ball. Tom Pritchard saw him there and held back a bit. Turning to go back to his mark, he said to Henry, fielding at mid off "Does he know who I am?"

"Yes" said Henry, "Ben's just told him." "He has, has he. I'll shift him," said Tom. He then proceeded to give the batsman a torrid time, but Major Towers never moved, taking every ball cleanly to the top of the stumps and flick to a fielder. Needless to say, he stood up to everyone all afternoon and there were no byes.

Later in the evening, we were having a drink and Tom Pritchard walked over when I happened to be with Major Towers. "Play much cricket?" he asked. "Oh, I expect I have about 6 or 7 games a season," said the immaculate keeper. "What a ******* waste," said Tom, and walked off.

It is incredible how some people have so much talent that is not used while others have so much enthusiasm but little ability, try as hard as they might.

There was an extraordinary player for Wolverhampton Chamber of Commerce in an evening match at Worfield. We were playing on the edge of the square, therefore there was a short boundary on one side. This fellow batted right handed one end and left handed at the other and pulled everything to the short boundary with great effect during his short innings. The only time I have ever seen this done!

FCCQ Question 12:
In Ashes Test Matches, W. Rhodes features in two record wicket partnerships. Which two?

A funny thing happened to us on the way to a Test Match at Trent Bridge. At 8.00 in the morning, Mike Fea was driving Ray and Dave Roberts and myself through Chapel Ash in Wolverhampton and Mike nearly went up the pavement. Walking down the street towards us was a trim young lady, and the only thing she was wearing was a wristwatch. As Mike said "It's quite a shock to the system at that time in a morning!" However, an event like that shortens the journey. That night, the local paper, the Express and Star, revealed that a patient from the nearby hospital had gone AWOL.

No, you weren't dreaming, Mike.

At Old Trafford, I remember the first ball Frank Tyson bowled after his exploits in Australia. He knew what was expected of him and a gasp went round the crowd as the ball thumped into Godfrey Evans gloves over his head standing a pitch length

FCCQ Question 13.
Malcolm Nash was the unfortunate bowler to be hit for six sixes by Gary Sobers. Name the bowler when Ravi Shastri repeated the feat.

back behind the stumps. Forget in swing or outswing, when anyone bowls that fast it can only go straight! It is not surprising Frank only had a short career – any player would soon burn out with all that effort. No doubt the fastest I ever saw, or didn't see, if you know what I mean!

Meanwhile, back at Edgbaston in another series, Tony Smout had eaten his way through the various packets of food marked 11 o'clock, Lunch, 3 o'clock, Tea, punctuated with apples, bananas and oranges, to say nothing of a few bottles of beer. Lance Gibbs had just come on for a new spell. Tony sat bolt upright and said, "He can't do that." "Can't do what?" we all asked. "He can't bowl that end after bowling at the other." Lance Gibbs had been bowling at the other end when Tony last saw him, but had dropped off to sleep and missed about four overs only to wake up to find the spinner had changed ends!

Mike Fea was driving to work one morning when, once again, he had a rude awakening. He was listening to Jack DeManio on the radio only to hear him say "Now I've got Marcus Thomas, skipper of Worfield Cricket Club, on the phone. Now, Marcus, tell me of this scheme of yours for a free night out." "Well, it's something the players have all agreed on and that is it seems unfair that, if a player gets a good score or takes a lot of wickets, he should have to buy a round of drinks. It would be much fairer the other way about." says Marcus. "And what are the new rules?" "They are as published in The Shropshire Star," said Marcus and went on to explain them as follows:

FCCQ Question 14:
Mark Robins holds the world record for failing to score in the most number of consecutive innings. How many?

1. Each player shall pay one shilling into "The Box", to be held by the last winner of a "Free Night Out". Should there be more than one winner, they share the Free Night Out. If there are more than two winners, the Free Night Out is void.

2. 2/6d of the Box funds shall go to Club Funds. If there is no winner of the "Free Night Out", all monies shall go to Club Funds.

3. To win a "Free Night Out", score 50 runs or more.

4. To win a "Free Night Out", take 7 wickets or more.

5. To win a "Free Night Out", hold 4 catches or more.

6. To win a "Free Night Out", take 5 wickets or more behind stumps.

7. To win a "Free Night Out", score 4 consecutive ducks.

8. The player holding "The Box" to be responsible for "waiting on" to the recipient of the "Free Night Out" and handing "The Box" over to the winner at the next match.

9. Winners to be recorded on the side of "The Box".

I believe this scheme worked successfully for about two seasons, and was fun while it lasted. I have to admit to being the only player to have a Free Night Out for failing to trouble the scorers on 4 successive occasions. I might add that it took me 12 weeks to achieve this, even though I played in every game. You never get in on a batsman's paradise at no. 11. Recorded in a Shropshire Star somewhere will also be the fact that I was also the first recipient by taking 8 wickets at Enville. It is nice to win, but more important to enjoy the game, whatever the result.

If you asked John Foster whether he was played for his batting

> FCCQ Question 15:
> Ian Botham holds the record for the most sixes in a season. How many?

or bowling, he would tell you "Neither, my transport!" He was one of the few owners of a Horseless Carriage in the early days. Nevertheless, John enjoyed a game and all that went with it. Having worked up a thirst at Enville, where the pubs closed half an hour earlier than in Shropshire, we called in at a crowded Six Ashes. "Not much room here" said John who, at 6' 8" was busy dodging the exposed ceiling joists. "We'll have to do something about this." and burst out singing the first verse of A Farmer's Boy. That did the trick – two tables suddenly cleared leaving us plenty of room. "Now, let's have a couple of plates of your excellent sandwiches, Fred," said John.

George Reece was Secretary of the Club when we moved to Davenport Park and did an awful lot of work in negotiating the site. However, he left shortly afterwards, taking a job in Gloucestershire. Some years later he was visiting and it was arranged for him to have a game. As we were getting changed, Denis Fincher said "Hey, George, do you remember when we put that kipper in Marcus' socks. Funny how he never said anything?" "He didn't say anything," said George, "Because they were *my* socks. I thought if I waited long enough I would find out the culprit, but I didn't think it would take 13 years."

There was a period when the ground was under attack from moles. Des Plain, the worthy treasurer of the club today became quite an expert catching them. One Sunday morning when we were about to leave the ground to

FCCQ Question 16:
Name the only bowler to have taken over 4,000 wickets in his career.

take lunch before the afternoon match, one of the players shouted "Hey Des, one of your traps has gone off" and, sure enough, within minutes of Des setting the traps, one went off as he was walking away from it. Des turned, took the trap out of the ground and raised it in the air shouting "Yes!" just like a bowler shouting "Howzat!" As he squeezed the trap, the mole dropped to the ground, ran across the turf and disappeared down the hole from whence he came. Poor Des – "Caught any moles lately?" was the usual greeting that weekend.

At the time when Mike Brearley first started wearing protective headgear, Bill Stocking went out to field with a motor cyclist's helmet on his head. He was fielding at mid wicket when the ball was spooned in his direction. He took off the helmet and held it out in both hands. The ball dropped nicely in and bounced out again! Ben Roberts was skipper at the time. "Get rid of that damn thing, Bill, you have given five runs away and given them an extra wicket." Bill got rid of the helmet and later said, "I didn't mind Ben telling me off I expected that, it was being sent to Coventry for the afternoon that got to me."

Tom Pitt had just come back from his exploits at Taunton where he played for Shropshire and scored 50 in 12 minutes off 15 balls. I met Tom in Bridgnorth and was just going to give him a lift home. He had his cricket gear with him, but his bat was loose.

I picked up his bat and said, "Is this the one that did the damage, Tom?" "Yeah, that's it," said Tom. "Toss one down" I said, handing him a table tennis ball that I had in my pocket from playing earlier that evening.

FCCQ Question 17:
Name the youngest player to score a double century in a first class cricket match.

Tom tossed the ball and with my No. 11 batsman's backlift, I hit Cowley's plate glass window. It went in and out like a Wobble Board and Tom shot round the corner like Linford Christie. The window had just stopped making Rolf Harris-like noises when Tom reappeared, poking his head round the corner and not another soul in sight. We bid a hasty retreat. "Difficult to assess a bat with a ping-pong ball, or a plate glass window, Tom." "Take my word for it, it's a good 'un." said Tom, "It's a good 'un." Incidentally, this is still a record for the fastest 50 in Minor County Cricket.

One weekend, George Reece had the misfortune to collect a king pair, both LBW. On the Saturday he was given out playing back and was advised he would have been better to have played that particular ball on the front foot. The next day, he went out, took guard and, to the first ball, planted his left leg firmly up the wicket only to be struck on the pad and be given out by the umpire. When he returned to the pavillion, he was greeted by Henry, the skipper, with "It looks like you can be given out LBW either forward or back, George." There was a stony silence until the next incident.

Bish was given run out, by a fortnight, and was greeted with the words "Not quite as quick as you used to be, Em." A further period of silence until play stopped for tea.
There was never any sympathy for what happened to you on the Cricket field, but, as regards other matters, they were the most caring fellows you could meet.

Tactfully, at tea, the LBW law and running between the wickets were not discussed! George was more preoccupied as

---

FCCQ Question 18:
Name the only batsman to score a double century twice in the same match.

---

to whether there was any more strawberry jam to go with the mountain of home made scones that he and Derek Brookes had started to consume.

Derek, a local farmer, was a big man with an appetite to match. His foreman was telling me how on one market day they called at a certain restaurant where Derek's eating capacity was well known to the chef who had vowed to 'Fix him'. Derek ordered a T-bone steak and, when it was served, it projected a couple of inches over both ends of the large oval plate. The chef observed from the kitchen doorway, but waved his hands in despair when Derek sent in for some more chips because there had not been enough room on the plate originally, due to the size of the steak!

Don't worry, Chef. He's got a lorry load of spuds outside.

FCCQ Question 19.
Name the only batsman to have scored over 400 twice.

THE 'NO BALL' ISSUE

I must take issue with Richie Benaud concerning the No Ball law. I am not sure in which year the law was changed, but it a long time now. Yet Richie still has a moan about it from time to time. So let's look at it in a logical manner.

Firstly, the object of the No Ball law is to prevent the fielding side taking an unfair advantage by the bowler getting too close to the batsman before releasing the ball.

Secondly, it is not essential for the umpire to call 'No Ball' quickly in order that the batsman has a free hit at the ball.

An immediate call is made in order that all players, both batsmen and fielders, are aware that the batsman cannot be given out on that delivery except in attempting a run and then he could be given 'Run out'. Remember, the batting side are awarded an extra run and another ball has to be bowled.

These two issues apply whichever No Ball law is applied.

Looking at the original rule first. From the position in which the umpire stands, it is impossible to administer this rule. That is, to look at the bowlers back foot and hand from which the ball is released at the same time. In the case of someone like Joel Garner, a distance in excess of eight feet! You might do it if you were cross-eyed, but then I'm not so sure.

The photograph of Harold Larwood's fine action shows the umpire watching his feet, but how he knows when the ball is released is difficult to say.

FCCQ Question 20:
Why was John Willes "No balled" in 1822?

The old rule meant that a bowler with a long delivery stride would land his front foot perhaps eighteen inches over the popping crease and it still be a legal ball. Eighteen inches nearer to the batsman, when bowling at 90 mph would reduce the time a batsman had to play the ball by a significant margin. The Bearded Wonder would, no doubt, provide a figure to the odd decimal place or two.

Digging a hole eighteen inches further up the pitch created uneven ground and caused a problem when batsmen took their stance at the crease.

With the front foot rule, the umpire can concentrate on the front foot. He can even observe this if required to stand close behind the stumps by the bowler.

The other umpire from square leg has the responsibility to watch the hand for 'throwing' and adjudicate the No Ball law concerning the number of fielders behind square on the leg side.

Another fine action shot, this time of none other than the great Richie Benaud himself about to deliver what would be a No Ball under the front foot law, yet his back foot is still behind the wicket – a large delivery stride for a bowler of his pace, but a good illustration of how a bowler could exploit the old law.

So much for the rules. I cannot for the life of me understand how bowlers constantly bowl No Balls when the solution is so simple.
Take the world class long jumper or triple jumper like Jonathon Edwards. It is absolutely vital to get the run up right so that the athlete lands right on the board for take off.

How does he do this? The run up is marked out accurately and when he starts from the right spot and his rhythm is good he knows he will hit the board right, without hesitation.

> *FCCQ Question 21:*
> *In which year was overarm bowling legalised?*

For a bowler to perform consistently, he must have a rhythmic approach to the wicket. In practice, I would then get the bowler to run to the wicket trying to bowl as fast as possible. Having then checked the distance he ran, I would make him start from that point and then using the same rhythmic approach to the wicket, say "Now let me see you bowl a No Ball starting from there."

If the same run up is used and the starting point is correctly placed, he will find it impossible to overstep.

With regard to First Class cricket, I would like to see a system adopted where bowlers run ups are identified by different coloured discs. Say red for Gough, blue for Cork, yellow for Caddick and so on. These would be placed at either end of the pitch prior to the start of each innings. This would achieve a number of benefits:

1.   The markers could be placed in position accurately, using measuring tape. This, I feel certain, should reduce the number of No Balls bowled

2.   It would save time during the match and a better over rate should be achieved.

3.   It would prevent scuff marks being made that can cause fielding errors and also prevent unnecessary work for the Groundsman.

As a matter of interest, who do you think was the bowler who caused most problems with his run up at Edgbaston according to Bernard Flack, the Head Groundsman at the time. I will give you a clue; he was a member of a touring party and bowled a great number of overs.
Another clue; he holds the record for the most consecutive Maiden overs

---

FCCQ Question 24:
If a player has not attempted to play the ball, is it possible for leg byes to be scored?

HAROLD LARWOOD IN ACTION

FCCQ Question 22:
Harold Larwood is still credited with an England record in Ashes Test Matches. What is it?

RICHIE BENAUD IN ACTION

FCCQ Question 23:
What Test Match record was Richie Benaud the
first player to achieve?

bowled in First Class cricket. That's him – Hugh Tayfield, or Toey Tayfield as he was known. Bernard said "he kicked Hell out of the wicket, that's when I first started putting cement in the mix to make good some of the holes overnight." Just think, sixteen consecutive Maidens, he could have bowled TWO complete stints in a limited overs game without conceding a single run. One hundred and thirty seven balls in all!

No doubt, in due course I will get Richie Benaud's view on the issue I have raised. However, the No Ball issue is also a major factor that the former Australian captain and I are in agreement about. The Slow over rate.

Six No Balls is the equivalent of an extra over being bowled, gifting at least 12 runs to the batting side under existing current laws, with an opportunity to double that with very little risk of losing a wicket.

> FCCQ Question 25:
> If the wicket keeper interferes with the batsman's right to hit the ball or defend his wicket, what should the umpire do?

As previously stated, laws should be about fair play, and in the professional game where fines are imposed, this should be equally true.

Any penalty clause for a slow over rate should be changed to a bonus/penalty clause, whereby players have the benefit of being paid for overs in excess of the mandatory over rate, in the same way as they can be penalised for not achieving the required standard. Incentive is the key.

Before embarking on such as scheme, I think, however, that it would be best to have a look at who is responsible for the slow over rate, I can assure you it does not rest entirely with the fielding side.

The batsmen are as much to blame as the bowlers. Batsmen frequently hold up play while the sight screen is moved, to tie a boot lace, change their bat or gloves, even the non striker can be guilty of holding up play while he removes or replaces his protective helmet and they are regularly having to pick up their bat or batting gloves that they have dropped in the process of dealing with their headgear.

So please, if it is necessary to impose financial penalties, be fair – share the blame and share the rewards.

It would be in the interests of all parties to think about the game a bit before going out at the start of each session, cut out the midfield conferences and get on with the game.

FCCQ Question 26:
What are the minimum and maximum weights of a top grade cricket ball?

Fine both sides for failing to meet standards and reward both sides when exceeding them. But, and there must be a but, set tough standards in the first place.

What do you think would be a fair over rate under these rules, Mr Benaud?

It is strange to me that a figure of twenty overs have to be bowled after the start of the last hour of play, yet fifteen overs per hour is acceptable prior to this.

The World Cup semi-final between Australia and South Africa that ended as a tied match threw up an interesting statistic.

South Africa bowled 6 no balls, gifting six runs and six extra balls to their opponents, whereas Australia did not bowl any no balls in this particular game.

I wonder what Bob Woolmer has to say about that!

FCCQ Question 27:
What width shall a pitch measure either side of a line joining the centre of the middle stump of both sets of wickets?

WHAT IS A WIDE?

The present day description reads:
"A wide is a ball bowled so high or so wide of the wicket that, in the opinion of the umpire, it passes out of reach of the striker standing in. a normal guard position. It must be called and signaled by the bowler's umpire as soon as it passes the lino of the striker's wicket."

There would appear to be two basic flaws in this law. One is that if a ball is bowled to a batsman like Tony Grieg, over 6ft 6in in height, he has a far greater reach than, say, Harry Pilling, at just over 5ft. This would mean that a ball bowled wide of the wicket to Tony Grieg may be seen as a legitimate ball, but would have been called wide to Harry Pilling.

The other problem is in the "opinion of the umpire" would the batsman have been able to have hit the ball had he moved his feet as opposed to not moving at all. To exaggerate the point a little, it would mean that a side bowling against a team of small men would have to bowl a much tighter line than against a team of giants. This is a great disadvantage, particularly in the limited overs game.

It seems wrong to me that there should be a different interpretation of the law on Wides for one day cricket and 3, 4 or 5 day games. As stated in the previous chapter, the object of the law is to maintain fair play and prevent one side having an advantage over the other.

The present No Ball rule achieves that, but the existing law on Wides is open to abuse by both sides. That is, deliberately

---

FCCQ Question 28:
Is it possible for a bowler to claim a wicket off a wide and, if so, name each way if more than one.

bowling wide to make it difficult for the batsman to score off the bowler. While, on the other hand, in the one day game, batsmen take up a certain stance at the wicket inviting the bowler to bowl down the leg side and refuse to play a shot, whereas, on other occasions, they would have pulled it over mid wicket.

The present rule is difficult for umpires to administer consistently, but there is a simple solution to this. My recommendation is for two new lines to be drawn 2ft 9in apart, centred on the middle stump and drawn at right angles between the wickets and the popping crease. Any ball that does not pass over this zone at some point of its journey through to the wicket keeper, would be deemed a wide in all forms of cricket. The stance the batsman took would have no influence over the umpire's decision and it would be an easy rule for the umpire to implement.

A batsman would be at liberty to hit a ball pitched outside these lines and thus make it into a legitimate delivery. It would only be balls that passed through to the wicket keeper without touching anything, or not passing through the 2ft 9in wide x 4ft long zone that would be called a wide ball.

At present, the batsman can be given out five ways off a wide: stumped, hit wicket, run out, handled ball or obstructed the field. It seems wrong to me that a player can be given out stumped off a wide ball as this means the bowler has bowled the ball out of the batsman's reach and the batsman has stepped out of his crease in an attempt to play the ball, thus giving an unfair advantage to the bowler.

FCCQ Question 29:
If a batsman is given out off a wide, are any runs scored?

Any of the other four reasons and the batsman would have no one to blame but himself or maybe his batting partner in the case of a run out.

I understand the reluctance to change laws that have been in operation for so many years, but it would be interesting to have the opinion of someone like Dickie Bird on these proposals. Now that Dickie has retired from International duty, he would be free to express an opinion and not be restricted or inhibited by any contract that a present member of the international panel of umpires might be.

Gamesmanship, as I understand it, is playing within the existing rules of the game, but, at the same time, exploiting any loop holes that provide an opportunity to benefit the cause, no matter how devious they may be, as long as they achieve the required result.

Sportsmanship, on the other hand, is playing within the spirit of the game at all times without the need to resort to devious methods.

No doubt, the vast majority of people would feel that it is in order to employ gamesmanship tactics against the Tax man but not on the cricket field. The difference here is that if the Tax Man discovers that you have found a loop hole in the tax laws, he very quickly amends them. I believe cricket administrators should adopt the same approach.

FCCQ Question 30:
How many ways is it possible to be out from a wide and name them.

THE MEN IN WHITE COATS

Give a man a white coat on a cricket field and extraordinary things can happen to a point where you think it might be necessary to send for two more men in white coats to take him away. However, they do a thankless job and also a very tiring one.

Like a good referee, a good umpire is hardly noticed. It is only when something controversial or amusing happens that they are noticed.

Spectators can be very partisan and often become deck chair critics. You can understand the feeling of a village umpire who had taken more than his fair share of criticism who, after giving an unpopular decision, walked over and sat in an empty deck chair and when asked what he thought he was doing, said "Oh, it seems pretty obvious you get a better view from here."

Some umpires can play to the gallery a little bit. Now take "Opple" for example – sorry, I can never remember his first name. He used to umpire at Hobsons. The louder a bowler appealed, the louder he would shout back "Not Out"– he nearly frightened young Geoff Roberts to death the first time he did it to him.

Bill Huson was a stalwart of Bridgnorth Cricket Club and a first class football referee. He coined the phrase "I'm in charge" long before Bruce Forsythe. Bill used to stand in the Bridgnorth K.O. and I often wondered how his decisions would stand up under the scrutiny of T.V. and a third umpire. It was incredible how often Bill would call a 'No Ball, thus awarding one side an extra run and two or three balls later call 'One Short' to take it off again to redress the situation.

FCCQ Question 31:
Who became the first overseas umpire to stand in a Test match in England?

My most recent grass roots umpiring incident happened last season. I went to watch two of my grandsons play in an evening match and was persuaded to umpire. My son-in-law, David, was umpiring the other end. When the first wicket fell on the penultimate ball of an over, Steven came out to bat. Taking guard he said, "Middle please, dad." "Oh hell!" Said the wicket keeper with a broad grin. Steven scored a single off the first ball received and prepared to face the next ball. "Middle please, grandad". The wicket keeper shouts, "That's it! Forget the appealing lads – you've no chance."

I played in a game with a Bridgnorth eleven at Wednesbury. It was a day match and it proved to be a good batting wicket, so the captains at lunch agreed to extend the hours of play from the original time of 6.30pm to 8.00pm. Tom Jenkins was the umpire and not at all, happy with that news. "They can't do that," he said, "6.30 is close of play in a day match." And it was. He said he had never seen a wicket deteriorate so much in the last hour of a day. If it hit the batsman on the pad, it was like Tony Greig says – "It was Goodnight, Charlie."

There are times when I have played in a game when the umpire is known to be finger happy and this can ruin a game. If this were the case, invariably the captain would ask you to watch what you were appealing for when bowling. It is not easy to edit your appeals, it is far better to play in a game where you know the batsman will get the benefit of the doubt. Mr. Fry at Cound was a very fair umpire, but I was able to use this to my advantage one day. I was bowling against "Tiger"

FCCQ Question 32:
Name the only umpire on the 1997 list of first class umpires never to have played first class cricket.

Roberts who had decided to play me off the front foot, mostly with his bat behind the pad. The first four balls all hit him on the pad without an appeal from Roy or me behind the stumps. The fifth ball, I cleared my throat with a good "Howzat" with not a word from Roy. Umpire Fry grins at me and says "You weren't serious were you, Eddie?" to which I replied "No, but he didn't know that." I bowled him next ball as he went on the back foot. "See what you mean," said Mr. Fry.

Herman Higgins umpired for Cleobury Mortimer. He had an artificial leg and used to sit on a shooting stick at square leg. Bish was batting and pulled a ball square: "Ping" it hit Herman on the leg and shot over the boundary and the umpire went base over apex. As everyone rushed over to him, he picked himself up and said, "Thank God it didn't hit my good'un!"

There was a fellow named Frank who used to come out from Wolverhampton and umpire for us, and very fair he was too. He was a bit of a mystery – he did not drive and we played at Acton Reynald one Saturday and at Caddesley Corbet the following day.

We asked him if he would like a lift, as they were both about 30 miles away, but in opposite directions to one another. "No, it will be alright, thanks" he said, "I will see you there." Each day, as we arrived, at the ground, he was walking up the last few yards to the entrance. We never saw anyone dropping him off or picking him up. He said, "My wife is a very temperamental woman", but we never met her. One day we went down to The Dog and Frank said "What are you having to drink; it's my wife's birthday and I'm having a bit of a celebration drink." The next night we went in again and Frank

---

FCCQ Question 33:
How many of the 1997 list of first class umpires were Test Players, and name them.

43

said, "What are you drinking? I made a bit of a mistake, it's my wife's birthday today, not yesterday!"

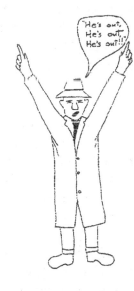

We were playing Quatt at Worfield one Saturday and the Rev. Jack Robinson of Quart and the Rev. Stanley Moore of Worfield agreed to stand as umpires. During the course of the game, Jack Evans was bowling for Quart and Ben Roberts was facing. Ben went down the wicket and took a swing to pull the ball to square leg where umpire Moore was standing.

Ben missed the ball, which went through to the wicket keeper, Cyril Link, who took the bails off with Ben well out of his crease. "Howzat" shouts Cyril only to find the umpire had turned his back on proceedings in taking evasive action. "Not out" he says, "I didn't see you take the bails off." Two balls later, Ben advances down the wicket again, this time the ball strikes Ben on the pad and before anyone could appeal, or thought about doing so, umpire Robinson raises both hands in the air with forefingers pointing skywards, and shouts, "He's out, He' s out, He's out!"

Divine Intervention

FCCQ Question 34:
Harold (Dicki Bird set a world record for number of tests in which he officiated before retiring from international duty. How many was it?

SINGLE WICKET COMPETITION

There is nothing worse than not having a game of cricket on a glorious summer weekend. If you are without a fixture for any reason, you can rest assured the weather will be the best you have had all season.

A Single Wicket competition could be your answer: it is simple to organise with 16 players being the ideal number, giving you 8 matches in the first round, 4 in the second, then the semi finals and the final. If you cannot muster 16 players, but have independent umpires, some players would have a bye in the first round and go straight into round two.

Sixteen names are drawn from a hat to provide you with the order for the first round of 8 matches. The competition then proceeds non-stop with players occupied as follows:

1 Batsman
1 Bowler
1 Runner - non striking batsman, who will be the next man in
1 Player padding up who will be the runner for the next innings
10 Fielders
2 Umpires

When the numbers are drawn out of the hat, there are two options; you can either draw them out two at a time and each pair toss a coin to see who bats first, or draw them out one by one and write them down in numerical order 1 – 16.

Eight players with the odd numbers bat first.

FCCQ Question 35:
In which year was the first Benson and Hedges Final held?

No 1 with No 3 as non striker

No 3 with No 5 as non striker

No 5 and so on until:

No 15 who has No 2 as non striker

No 2 with No 4, etc., etc.

When the first round matches have been completed, it is a good time to have a break. Put all the eight winners' names in a hat and repeat the process for the second round and semi finals.

The first two umpires will be batsmen numbers 15 and 16 for the first four matches and the losers from matches 1 and 2 for the next four games.

For the second round matches, the umpires will be the losers of matches 3 and 4.

The semi finals and final to be umpired by two volunteers most suited for the job.

The innings will consist of two overs, one to be bowled from each end, or at the fall of a wicket, whichever occurs first. The same format with regard to batsmen and runners to be followed for the second round as in the first; that is for the batsman of the following innings to act as runner.

For the semi final and final, the batsmen will be free to select their own volunteer runners. The final to consist of 4 overs,

---

FCCQ Question 36:
Name the winners of the first Benson and Hedges Cup Final.

each bowl 2 from each end, unless, of course, a wicket is taken. All normal cricket laws apply with the exception that if the runner or non striking batsman is run out, the batsman at the other end loses his wicket and the innings is, therefore, closed.

This form of competition is an excellent form of practice, in that every player is involved with every aspect of the game.
That is:
1. Umpiring – brush up on the laws and signals
2. Batting
3. Bowling
4. Fielding
5. Captaincy
6. Field Placing
7. Observing other players strengths and weaknesses
8. Running between the wickets

A keen member of a side will know the strengths and weaknesses of his fellow players, but will he be able to exploit them to his advantage. Will he also know where to place various players in the field, the mobile ones and the less mobile, etc. etc.

Round One is 8 matches of four overs, that is 32 overs if required. Experience suggests that only two thirds of these will be used, so that would reduce it to about 20 overs.

Round Two is 4 matches of four overs, that is 16 overs possibly reduced to 12, the Semi finals being two matches of 4 overs. So this will occupy about 40 overs prior to the Final.

FCCQ Question 37:
In which year was the first Gillette Cup Final?

Now, to make it really interesting, you can have a competition within a competition. If you have anyone who is prepared to run a book, you can have someone, like Johnners used to say, "Here comes Godders with the Odders from Ladders."

One would normally expect an all rounder to do well in this form of competition, but there can be some surprise results. A competition for the best fielder is a good idea. There is always the question of whether a particular ball offered a chance or not. Some fielders do not attempt to make catches whereas others turn what looks to be impossible into a good catch.

The same can be said with regard to ground fielding, and failing to cut off shots to the boundary.

The fairest way to assess this situation is a consensus of opinion by the other fielders. I reckon this could be signaled to the umpire and, via him, to the scorer. I therefore propose two new umpire signals:

> 1. A pair of praying hands for a missed catch, with all due respect to Rev. David Shepard and stories related to him and Fred Trueman
>
> 2. A hand over the eyes – in the "I didn't see it" or "Where is it?" stance

---

FCCQ Question 38:
Name the winners of the first Gillette Cup Final.

THE AMATEUR SELECTOR

Before every Test Match for one day internationals, we all have our own ideas of the players we would pick or leave out for the next important match. Rarely do we agree with the final decision.

My personal view is that 5 top order batsman plus a wicket keeper should be capable of scoring enough runs to enable a good bowling side of five varied bowlers to bowl them out for less.

Players should bat in the normal position that they normally play for their county. Where possible a right and left handed pair should open the batting, as this does seem to cause problems for a high percentage of opening bowlers and, of course, the need for changes in field placings.

At international level, batsmen should be able to bat on any type of wicket and against any type of bowling. Bowlers should be able to bowl on any type of wicket. A greater degree of accuracy is obviously required on a good batting surface.

I would always pick two opening bowlers, one an out and out paceman and one with the ability to use he new ball to good effect as would a first change bowler.

My policy would always be to pick the best available wicket keeper who would be expected to bat at no.6 unless, of course, one of the five bowlers thought to be more proficient with the bat than the keeper.

FCCQ Question 39:
Name the player to hold the record for the most wickets in a Test Match series and state how many.

Fielding is also a consideration and, therefore, when two candidates for a particular position in the side are of equal status in batting or bowling ability, the better fielder would be preferred.

There is no other game in the world that I know of where the captain has such an influence on the outcome of a game.

The ability to win the toss of a coin is not the greatest requirement; in fact, there have been many times when a captain would be happy for his opposite number to have to make the decision to bat or bowl.

Captaincy is about getting the best out of each and every member of the side and to do this it may be necessary to bully one player, plead with another, urge another and keep them all involved and let them know they have their part to play.

The introduction of covered wickets has reduced the need for the fully balanced side that I have suggested, which is a great shame.

The West Indies sides with a battery of four fast bowlers has proved effective, but this would not have been the case if the wickets at some time in the matches hand been reduced to a soft pudding by exposure to rain. When this was the case, they managed to produce such bowlers as Ramadin and Valentine and then Lance Gibbs, the only off-spinner to take over 300 test wickets.

FCCQ Question 40:
Name the player who scored the most runs for England in a Test Match series and state how many.

From the players available at that time, I think the best balanced English side I can recall was:

Peter Richardson	Cohn Cowdrey
David Shepherd	Peter May
Tom Graveney	Trevor Bailey
Godfrey Evans	Jim Laker
Tony Lock	Fred Truman
Brian Statham	

On a rainy day, picking various teams could be fun. Taking a letter from the alphabet for surnames. For example, would you bet on the B, G or S when you consider the sides listed below.

Boycott	Gooch	Stolmeyer
Barber	Grenidge	Simpson
Barrington	Gavaskar	Sharpe
Bradman	Gatting	Smith M J K
Barlow	Gower	Smith R
Botham	Graveney	Sobers
Bailey	Grout	Stewart
Bairstow	Garner	Shastri
Benaud	Griffiths	Snow
Boyce	Gifford	Small
Brown	Gibbs	Statham

When it comes to one day cricket, I am still of the opinion that a well balanced bowling attack is favourite. There are very few batsman who can maintain their momentum against both quick and

---

FCCQ Question 41:
Name the player to score the most Test Match centuries in his career and state how many.

---

slow bowling without making a mistake or two.

The very best players should be able to play one or five day cricket equally well. How do you think Denis Compton or Keith Miller would have performed in the one day game, and I think Tony Lock would have been in his element.

A topic of convoroation that has been raised many times and particularly on wet days, when cricketers at all levels discuss the all time great players is:
What would be best eleven England could field selecting players from all generations past and present.

I have selected an exclusive eleven on qualification only. Sorry, but there is no place for Sir Jack Hobbs, Herbert Suttcliffe, Denis Compton, Geof Boycott, Harold Larwood or Jim Laker.

The select band to qualify are:

Len Hutton	Graham Gooch	John Edrich
Wally Hammond	Andy Sullivan	Frank Wooley
Les Ames	Ian Botham	Fred Truman
Titch Freeman	Bob Willis	12th man W G Grace

The first seven players have all scored over a hundred first class centuries.
The first five batsman have all scored test match triple centuries. Frank Wooley, as the all rounder, did the double of 2000 runs and 100 wickets on 4 occasions.

FCCQ Question 42:
Name the only player to have taken two hat tricks in Test Matches.

Les Ames is the only wickets keeper to score 100 centuries and also the only keeper to claim over 100 wickets in a single season.

Fred Truman, Bob Willis and Ian Botham have all taken over 300 test wickets. Titch Freeman is the only bowler to take over 300 wickets in a season.

I think W. G. would be a bit peeved at being 12th man as he has similar credentials to Frank Wooley. However, Frank was a left hand bat and bowler. W. G would be useful cover if either of the openers got crocked and I suppose he could always do the Physio's job.

Botham at no.8 would rarely get a knock, so he would have a point to prove when he did.

The first seven players have a combined average of 45.22 per innings, which means at the fall of the sixth wickets, you could expect 316 runs on the board each innings.

Titch Freeman would be able to bowl one end all day, which he loved.

The fast bowlers would only need short spells and would therefore always be fresh. I don't think Hammond or Gooch would be required to bowl much.

It has often been said that Denis Compton's generation lost some of their best years during the Second World War. This is true, but the same could be said for Frank Wooley and the First World War.

FCCQ Question 43.
Name the only county side to win a first class, two innings, match, without losing a wicket.

Being an amateur selector can be fun. You have a go.

Pick an eleven from the rest of the world to play my select 300 club" side with at least one player from each of the Test playing nations.

Australia

India

Pakistan

New Zealand

West Indies

Sri Lanka

South Africa

Zimbabwe

FCCQ Question 44:
Name the only side to have ten different fielders hold a catch in one innings of a first class match.

A TRIBUTE TO D.C.S. COMPTON ON ST GEORGE'S DAY

A sporting hero died today

Mine and a million others I dare say

Denis Charles Scott Compton were his names

Cricket and Football were his games.

He played both games with a grin

Any other way would have been a sin.

Eighteen centuries in a season

Just for fun, no other reason.

His brother, Leslie, played as well

Both for Middlesex and Arsenal.

The F.A. Cup Final and he felt sick

But a halftime brandy did the trick

A double international he became

And with that, a household name

The original Sporting Star

Adored by all, near and far

FCCQ Question 45:
Denis Compton 's highest first class innings was 300 runs.
How long did it take him to complete this treble century?

"The Brylcream Boy" as he was known

From boards and buses his face was shown.

Fame and adoration did no harm

Denis always retained his charm

He was without doubt a ladies man

But without trying as others can

A long cricket career was not to be

Stopped in his prime by "The Compton Knee"

A journalist and TV pundit he became

His approach to this was just the same

To him, watching cricket was still a joy

Just the same as when but a boy.

Sport for enjoyment, but always fair

Especially when played with the Compton Flair.

FCCQ Question 46:
Don Bradman scored his 100th century in 297 innings. How many innings did it take Denis Compton to achieve the same feat?

OTHER GRASS ROOTS

Alveley Cricket Club provided the venue for Worfield's first century maker and it was fitting that it should be the Club captain, Henry Seedhouse, who, in storybook fashion, happened to be the village Blacksmith. Alveley batted first and scored in excess of two hundred runs by tea.

The Alveley captain came into our dressing room before taking his side out to field and said "I'm sorry, Henry, I know you're not up to strength today." That was because two of our players, Marcus and Ben, had gone on a tour with our arch-rivals, Claverley. "Cheeky Sod!" said Henry, "We'll show 'em." and strode purposefully to the wicket. 105 runs later, he was out, but with the game virtually won. George Reece and Henry Yates saw us past their total. In fairness to the Alveley captain, Robin France, he was first down the wicket to congratulate Henry.

It was a Captain's innings and no mistake, but I often wondered how much Robin France's remarks were responsible for Henry's century that day. I understand Henry' s son, Michael, scored a century on the same ground exactly twenty years later. Now Michael's son, Ian, has passed the magical three figure mark on several occasions.

I am not in a position to ask The Bearded Wonder or Wendy Wimbush for ball by ball information, so there is no intention to provide statistical information. However, two matches at Acton Reynold, specific details come to mind. Against the bowling of Brian Perry, who played Minor Counties cricket for Shropshire, Norman (Sam) Perry and Marcus Thomas put on 176 runs for the first wicket.

FCCQ Question 47:
What is the highest 10th wicket partnership in the Nat West Trophy, and by whom?

Sam got off the mark with a six over the sight screen behind the bowler, they ran a leg bye off the next and Marcus pulled the next for six over square leg. Both were out in the nineties. In the other game, Roy Buck claimed six victims behind the stumps, all off my bowling, four caught and two stumped.

I am sad to say that neither Apley or AT&E grounds are in existence today. There are not enough young folk to sustain a side at Apley and the AT & E ground is now a housing estate.

Claverley, being our neighbouring parish, were also our deadly rivals. On one occasion, we beat them by nine wickets by tea time. After such humiliation, they did not want to play a limited overs game afterwards, as would normally be the case. Instead, we visited the top, the middle and the bottom pubs in the village to make sure the locals got the story right.

After this, I adjourned to the Swancote Country Club, where a dance was being held for Peter Walker's benefit. Glamorgan were due to play Claverley on the Sunday. I met up with Don Sheppard and Ozzie Wheatley, who took great pleasure in asking every Claverley player they saw if they had bought me a drink yet. Quite a night!

Incidentally, it is only somewhere like Claverley that could produce someone to go on the television programme "What's my Line". Godfrey Booth beat the panel as, wait for it, "A cag handed straw wimbler." Oh, I nearly forgot – Bridgnorth sent George Hawker, who also beat the panel as "A pork pie raiser."

FCCQ Question 48:
Name the only father and son to score centuries in the same first class innings

---

Burwarton is a nice picturesque spot, but not on the day Bernard Flack turned up as a guest player for us. It was raining "cats and dogs" and when Henry Yates turned up towing a trailer with a sow in it, we realised it was off for the day. Henry reckoned he would be better employed introducing his passenger to his dad's prize boar.

Sadly Blymhill and Weston Cricket Club no longer exists. We played there one beautiful, hot day and Jack Turner, a Brewery representative with a physique to match, scored 76 in 7 innings – well he was dropped 7 times. When he was eventually caught, he was heard to say, "Thank God for that." He was still sweating when we parted company at 11.00pm.

Willey is a lovely rural setting and it was there one day I witnessed what can only be described as an electric piece of fielding. Jack Chatham was the fielder; he was in the deep and the ball was skied in his direction. He started to run towards it when both of his feet slid from under him, but he was back on his feet in a flash, the ball dropping where he had been lying a split second earlier.

Through a cloud of smoke, he picked up the ball and threw it in while everyone else was rocking with laughter. He had had a full box of matches in his back pocket and they had all ignited as he hit the turf. To say he had rosy cheeks is somewhat of an understatement.

FCCQ Question 49:
Name the youngest player to score 50 first class centuries

Middleton Scriven was a small ground and we were happy to bowl them out for 50 runs. The chances of one of our players scoring a half century looked slim, but cricket has that unique ability to produce the unexpected. Ken Reece scored one not out and Henry Seedhouse scored 50 not out, as we won by ten wickets.

Incidentally, on the same day Bill Davies caught a House Martin one handed as it flew out of its pavilion nest.

Neenton Bashers, now there is a name to conjure with, a team of nomad farmers that we played in the Broseley Knockout. As the teams arrived at the ground, the captains tossed up and our skipper decided we would bat first. Then the news came through that a car had turned over and four of their players were delayed. We decided to provide them with four subs until these players arrived.

The subs were changed as wickets fell and our players were required to go in and bat and our fielders took six superb catches to help dismiss our own side for less than 100. Just as our last wicket fell, the four missing players turned up.

Those four Neenton Bashers lived up to their names and proceeded to bash the runs off in double quick time. Exit Worfield. I would like to think that the present generation would provide four subs, but would have better luck with their bowling.

There was a period when we had return fixtures with Welshpool, played on the May and August Bank Holidays. On one occasion, we had a coach to Welshpool to play a day

FCCQ Question 50:
Name the oldest player to captain England

match – it was a glorious morning and developed into a boiling hot day. It was agreed that we would play for a 9 gallon barrel of beer.

Welshpool batted first and scored around 320 all out; we then batted and I joined Ken Reece, one of the opening batsmen, at a point when all four results were possible. I had been offered a pint of beer before I went in to bat as last man, but I took the matter seriously and declined. Ken and I managed to put the 300 up, but fell 15 short of the total required when stumps were drawn, and the match ended as a draw.

It had been a good day's cricket - over 600 runs scored and 19 wickets fell. On returning to the pavilion I said "I can do with that pint now" but I was already too late – they had already drunk the 9 gallons.

As we left the field to hold the usual post mortem at "The Angel Inn", a thunderstorm broke out and the pub was in darkness, the lightening had caused a power cut. The lads had started chanting "Why are we waiting, why are we waiting" as no one had a drink at that time. However, as I walked in, the Landlord appeared with a lovely pint of bitter and said "There you are, Eddie, you have earned that, it's on the house, I made the B*****s wait."

We left Welshpool in good spirits and the thunderstorm followed us all the way back to Worfield. As we walked into "The Dog" the lights went out again and out came the candles. However, there was no problem in pulling a pint of beer, there were no electric engines in those days!
I could not say what time we left the candlelit hostlery, but it was a very long storm and, as old Walter the Landlord said, you couldn't expect a fellow to go out in weather like that or sit all night in a pub without a drink in his hand.

"The Dog" was the venue for many a team's dart match when games

FCCQ Question 51:
Brian Close 's test career spanned 27 years. How many England caps was he awarded in this time?

were rained off. 1001 up, a double to start and finish, eleven to a side. Getting the batting order right was important, knowing when to cheer and when to call for silence was an important factor. There was usually a gallon jug of bitter being passed round and filled at regular intervals, the losing side paying for the contents. I do not recall having to pay out; although I do not profess to be a darts player, I was normally called upon before the double to finish was required.

Bridgnorth cricket ground was the scene of many an interesting game in their Knockout competitions. There was one game when Henry Seelhouse and Ben Roberts, both over 40 years of age, ran two 5's in one over. It makes your legs ache to think about it.

Bridgnorth had "The Black Shed Boys", the local wags who watched every game with shouts like "Give him a bucket" when anyone dropped a skier. I remember being under a skier one night, you know the type where you could have drunk a pint of bitter while you were waiting for it come out of orbit, right in front of the pavilion. "He'll drop this, he's no chance" and then Freda Bishop's voice to top them all "Course he'll catch it." I dared not drop it then. Thankfully, I held onto it. "That's the way to shut 'em up, Eddie," she shouted, "Next, please."

FCCQ Question 52:
Name the only player to do the double of 2000 runs and 200 wickets in a first class season

One of the most exciting games we played in ths K.O. was against Alveley, regular winners of the competition at that time. There were no restrictions on the number of overs a bowler could bowl, so it was commonplace for two bowlers to bowl ten overs each. Alveley batted first and scored 139 in twenty overs, which is a big score to chase, particularly against the pair of opening bowlers recognised as the best in the area, Les Jones and Doug Westwood.

At this juncture, Walter Eccleston, our local Landlord, and Doug Clark, one of our supporters, had a wager of a bottle of Scotch, one saying we would get the runs required and the other that we would not. Sam Perry and Marcus Thomas went out to open the innings. The first ball went straight back past the bowler faster than it had left him – 4 runs – the chase was on! It came down to the last over.

Marcus was still in, but we had lost 4 wickets at the other end. By this time, Walter and Doug had drunk one bottle of Scotch. On the penultimate ball of the over, we lost another wicket. Bish went out to face the last ball – one run to tie, two to win. Marcus went to meet him. "Look, Bish, whatever happens, I'm coming for the last run." "OK, it's up to you" said Bish. He took guard, the bowler came in – CRACK! – 4 runs past point. Bat under arm, Bish walked off, Marcus ran for cover.

Walter and Doug finished the second bottle. "Damn good win, that" they said, although how much they saw we will never know, as they could not remember what the bet was in the first place, they adjourned to "The Dog."

At Cound there was some poor fellow who we understood had

FCCQ Question 53:
Name the only bowler to achieve a hat trick with three stumpings

been batting well in previous matches. However, today was not to be his day. Run out without facing, a direct hit, suicidal run. He was not pleased. Then we heard the bat hit the back of the pavilion and within seconds a gun shot – BANG ! The timing was perfect, the shot had in fact come from a farmer's shotgun in a neighbouring field. The batsman appeared in the doorway, but did not appreciate the reason why everyone was laughing

Cleobury Mortimer has always been an enjoyable fixture and Marcus invited a newcomer to the parish to play for us there one Saturday. Christiansen this fellow was called, and we advised him about our run out specialist. The Denis Compton of our club, Edwin Golden We warned him to watch it if he was batting with Edwin, he'd run pretty well everyone in the club out. Now "Chris" as he was known said "It is no problem, all you have to do is say no." "You have been warned" we said. Sure enough, Edwin was the non-striking batsman when Chris went out to bat. He took guard, played the first two balls with a dead bat – no problem so far.

The third ball he played into the covers "Yes" he called, starting to run down the wicket. "No," said Edwin, holding up his hand and not moving out of his crease. Chris never got back. It did not help matters when he returned to the pavilion to find us all grinning, but not a word was spoken.

It was a journey back from Cleobury Mortimer that produced my favourite story. We were travelling in convoy and George Reece ran out of petrol in his van. We all pulled up and someone produced some plastic tubing and John Adams, who had two little girls, produced a child's potty. Bish syphoned

---

FCCQ Question 54:
Name the only wicket keeper to claim a hat trick of stumpings

---

some petrol out of one of the other vehicles into the potty and was just pouring the contents into George's van when the local vicar passed by on his bike. He looked across and shouted, "I wish I had your faith!"

With the name of Bishop, he stood a better chance than the rest of us!

Jack Breakwell, whose son Denis played for Somerset, was a very good club cricketer who had scored more than one century against us. We therefore delighted when we played at Hobsons and he came out to open the batting with the skipper and he was run out without facing because he jogged the first run and had his wicket thrown down by Alan Tysdale. Roy Buck and I turned to one another and both said "Guess who will be opening the bowling for Hobsons." When they went out to field, we heard the skipper say, "Will that end be alright for you, Jack?"
John A Smith played us in the Express and Star Knockout. Edwin opened the bowling and his first ball caught the edge of the bat, hit a pad, removed the off bail and Roy caught the ball behind the wickets.

> FCCQ Question 55:
> Name the only player to be given out "obstructed the field" in a test match

The batsman then stepped back and flattened all three stumps. The batsman stopped and put the stumps back up and the bails on, and we thought it was a very sporting gesture. However, he then took guard again. "Sorry, but you're out, mate." said Marcus, our skipper. "That ain't jonnuch" said the batsman, "Not first ball" as he reluctantly returned to the pavilion.

Now, if anyone at Worfield Cricket Club is not too happy with anything, you will hear the expression "That ain't jonnuch".

We played at Knockin in a snowstorm. Edwin was bowling and I was fielding in the slips with Dave Roberts, our other opening bowler, who was due to bowl the next over. I said to him "My hands are that cold I cannot feel a thing, so don't expect me to catch anything." Would you believe the very first ball he bowled flew off the edge of the bat into my hands and out again. The rest of the players could not understand it when Dave stood in the middle of the pitch laughing.

FCCQ Question 56:
Name the England captain when England lost to New Zealand for the very first time

66

SIX A SIDE TOURNAMENTS

The six a side format that Worfield C.C. have employed over the last few years is described in this chapter.

There are twelve sides in this invitation knock-out competition. In the first two rounds there are two groups with six sides in each group. Every team plays three matches in the first round. This, in turn, produces a league table with a winner and runnerup from each group going into the knock-out semi-final stages of the competition.

The final is increased to 5 overs per side so that the fifth player and, presumably, the weakest link in the bowling element of the side also has to bowl an over.

The basic rules are as follows:
1.   All teams must be properly dressed in full Cricket attire.
2.   The wicket-keeper must wear wicket-keeping pads and gloves at all times when fielding.
3.   First and second round matches to consist of four six ball overs per side, bowlers to be restricted to one over per game.
4.   In the first round matches, all players must open the batting in at least one match so that there will be three different pairs of batsmen for each side represented.
5.   Each team must be ready to take the field within two minutes of the specified time or risk being "timed out" and the match awarded to their opponents who will be awarded points.
6.   In the event of 5 wickets falling, the last batsman will bat on while the last player to lose his wicket remains at the

FCCQ Question 57:
Name the county that holds the record for the lowest innings total and state that total

67

wicket as a non striker batsman. Should the non striker be run out, the last player loses his wicket.

The play is continuous. The first ball is bowled at 10.00 a m and, with luck, the last one about 8.00 p m.

Len Ball, the current Club Secretary, has devised his own method of charting the results that works very well and that is by using different coloured pens for each of the three matches that form a round for each group.

Match 1. A & B marked in Red
C & D marked in Blue
E & F marked in Green

A & C marked in Red
B & D marked in Blue

In order to keep teams informed of events, it is necessary to display a chart recording results and points scored after each match.

It is also essential to have two official scorers to tabulate events as they occur.

A well-manned scoreboard is also necessary to keep both players and public informed of the up-to-date situation of each and every match.

To any club contemplating running such a tournament, it is essential that you have the following personnel available:

FCCQ Question 58:
Name the county that holds the record for the highest innings total and state that total

---

1. A club official to mastermind events and chart results as they happen.
2. Caterers to provide lunch and tea for about 100 people and any additional guests.
3. Umpires panel – minimum of six.
4. Minimum of two official scorers.
5. Minimum of two scoreboard operators.
6. Bar staff to continually operate the bar.

In order to follow the order of events, substitute your own twelve teams for the teams used for illustration purposes below:

GROUP A	GROUP B
Black	Little
White	Large
Brown	Small
Green	Stout
Gray	Short
Gold	Long

Group A play all odd numbered matches and Group B all even numbered matches with the innings of each game sandwiched between each other.

FCCQ Question 59:
Name the only Englishman to score 6 successive hundreds

Match No

1 Black v Brown	
2	Little v Small
3 White v Green	
4	Large v Short
5 Gray v Gold	
6	Stout v Long
7 White v Black	
8	Large v Little
9 Brown v Gray	
10	Small v Stout
11 Gold v Green	
12	Long v Short
13 Black v Gray	
14	Small v Large
15 White v Gold	
16	Little v long
17 Brown v Green	
18	Stout v Short

19 Winner of Group A v Runner-up of Group B

20 Winner of Group B v Runner-up of Group A

21 FINAL

Winner of Match 19 v Winner of Match 20

In the Final, 5 Overs per side are bowled and all other rules apply.

FCCQ Question 60:
Name the only player, other than wicket keepers, that has taken over 1000 catches in his career

A NAME DROPPING TRIP TO LILESHALL

This description of the trp includes a special quiz question and also a number of first class cricketers names from all generations and varied nationalities, either listed or hidden in the dialogue. The answer to the quiz question and the cricketers names can be found at the back of the book

As an introduction to indoor cricket, I thought it would be a best for my friends to pay a visit to Lileshall and watch a game being played.
Before setting off on our journey, I reflected on how things had changed from when my brother and I first started work.

I used to cycle in to Bridgnorth to catch a bus to Kidderminster and my brother cycled down to catch a bus at the wheel to Chapel Ash in Wolverhampton. Sometimes he would have to walk to Compton in order to get on the bus to come home. That was until he got to know the regular drivers and conductors, he used to wait a little further on down past the crowded bus stop and the driver would slow down so that he could hop onto the platform at the rear of the bus.

Where Swancote country club is now, used to be the home of the Gray family.

Now, the bus that was due in Bridgnorth at 6.00 p.m. used to drive in one entrance of the drive to the house and out the other, picking David Gray up at the front door on route. The last bus back to Wolverhampton at night used to reverse the trip, dropping David off at his home front door.

Incidentally, it was not unusual for that last bus to stop off at a farm near Red Hill and have a fry-up of home cured bacon and free-range eggs for supper before returning to the depot. David Gray's brother, Claud, was

> *FCCQ Question 61:*
> *Name the Englishman to score the most scores of over 200 and state how many.*

telling me of one occasion when his brother had been dropped off one night when it was raining" stair rods" and David had had more than" one over the eight" and Claud watched from his own bedroom window.

David got his keys out and negotiated the steps to the front door. Just as he was about to put the key in the lock, he lost his balance and fell back into the bushes in the forecourt. He picked himself up and came up the steps and tried again. At the same point he lost his balance and down he went again into the bushes. He got up, shook himself like a dog, and tried again and for the third time finished up in the bushes. By this time he was like a drowned rat. However, he picked himself up again, paused at the bottom step, turned and then came up the steps backwards, then turned and surprised the lock by inserting the key and falling through the open doorway.

I asked Claud why he didn't go and help him. "What, and miss all the entertainment. He was wet anyway and he had always managed to get in before" he said.

Although I live in North Wales, I am still in regular contact with my old club in Shropshire and visit the area whatever I can to look up many friends and a few relatives.

Setting off from Rhos-on-Sea, the original home of Wilfred Wooler, that stalwart of Glamorgan and Welsh cricket in general. It was going to be a round trip but well worth it if it meant meeting up with some of my old cricketing comrades.

FCCQ Question 62:
Name the bowler to take the most Hat tricks in his career and state how many

My wife, Lily, said I ought to take a trip to the barber, but I said that I preferred not to have my hair too short at that time of the year and the weather forecasters had predicted more snow. Anyway I did not have time, as I had to drop a parcel off in Conway for our son, Douglas. Pick up Bill in Mold and Andrew in Flint before going on to Shrewsbury. "Well perhaps you will have a word with the contractor before you go. It is time they had finished. The tiler as only got one wall to grout and the carpenter to fix that banister in the hall" said my wife. OK, OK" said I, "anything for a quiet life."

So many things had been going round in my brain. Not to forget some flowers and a valentine card and collect my suit from the tailor. My wife called out again, "If you want me to cook you a meal when you get back, you had better fetch a leg of lamb from the butcher." "I'll do that right away," I said, "but I will be on my way then, as things are getting to close for comfort if I am to pick my friends up on time."

I got into the car and tuned onto Test Match Special. Would you believe it, it was raining again. So Jeremy Coney was talking to Jonathan Agnew prior to the third test with New Zealand. England had retained the same side as for the second test. It was: Knight, Atherton, Stewart, Hussain, Thorpe, Crawley, Cork, Croft, Gough, Caddick and Tufnell.

Quite a good balanced side that, although personally, I thought it very hard on Jack Russell, world record holder for the most wickets behind the stumps in a test match, batted like a hero in South Africa, had done nothing wrong. He would have been another left-handed in the side to make it awkward for the

FCCQ Question 63:
Name the fielder to take the most catches in a match and state how many.

fielding side. There was no doubt that Alec Stewart had earned his place for his batting alone, but he is not a natural wicket-keeper and motivator like Jack Russell or Alan Knott. Sorry John Crawley, but if I had been picking the side you would have been twelfth man for Jack to keep wicket.

John Bracewell came on the air, New Zealand were still to announce their side, but no, Richard Hadlee was not making a comeback.

I stopped to pick up my first passenger and was pleased to note he had a number of newspapers under his arm so we would be able to read what Gower, Benaud and Boycott had written or not written as the case may be.
As we carried on with our journey, Bill said "As daft as you like April will be over in four weeks and the English cricket season will be under way again".

All of a sudden, traffic was reduced to a crawl, yet we could not see what was holding us back. First we thought it was an old bus, then we discovered it was a low-loader. Fortunately, we were able to turn off and thus avoid traveling in a convoy for miles. I wanted to see my brother-in-law at Gabowen hospital, hence the reason for our diversion.

I quickly saw the nurse on the ward only to be told there had been a bit of a hick-up and that John had not been admitted after all. I thanked the little darling, and we were on our way again.

Being on familiar territory now, I was able to take a short cut down a lane over a bailey bridge spanning a brook and finally

---

FCCQ Question 64:
Name the wicket keeper to make the most dismissals in a season and state how many.

---

back out into the high street at Oswestry. We were not long getting to Shrewsbury where we stopped for a bite to eat.

As I paused outside the Lion Hotel to lock the car, my pals studied the menu. "Take your pick," said Bill, "Eddy is paying." "In that case, it's coffee and cake. If you want to go wild, that's up to you and will also be down to you," I said. "No, one of Johnner's cream cakes and a drink will do for me," said Andrew.

Shrewsbury was a convenient stop to take a break, but the main reason was for Bill to meet his sister, a Miss Grace Mailey, and pass on some tickets for "Julius Caesar". She was an avid theatre goer – the last time we met, she had just been to see an amateur production of "The King and I".

As we walked through the reception, Andrew was asked if he would be staying for one or two nights. Which reminds me of the story when Alec Bedser and Jack Crapp were rooming together and Jack was first to arrive at reception to be greeted with the question" Bed, sir?" To which Jack replied "No, Crapp." "Oh! first door on the right," said the receptionist. Sorry I digress, and that sounds like Ronnie Corbett and his arm chair shaggy dog story role.

Whilst taking our refreshments, conversation turned to next winters tour of the West Indies and whether it would be possible to fly by Virgin or Laker by the time the tour started. To cricket widows, the sound of Jamaica or Barbados has a certain romantic appeal. Time flies when you are talking about holidays, so we bade a hasty farewell and continued on our journey.

FCCQ Question 65:
Who broke W Edrich & D Compton's record for 3rd wicket stand in 1997?

---

as we headed towards Newport, I said, "Now I have a good quiz question for you two to answer before we get to Lilleshall. Name the only player to have had six consecutive sixes scored off his bowling in first class cricket in England".

"Fair enough," said Bill, "Malcolm Nash was in Wales when Gary Sobers hit his six sixes and Ravi Shastri was in India when he did it."
"I will give you a clue, he was a left arm spinner" I said. "Wardle," "no, Bob Berry". "No".
"I couldn't see anyone doing it to Underwood"said Andrew. The car went quiet for a spell as my pals tried to recall the name of some unfortunate bowler.
"Ray East," "No, I'm sorry"
"John Childs," "No".
"Nobody returned the compliment on Sobers, did they?" "That's a thought, but still no."
"Phil Edmonds," "No".
"Look, I will give you another clue," I said, "The batsman was an overseas player". " That's a big help," said Bill. "When you consider every county now has one, including Yorkshire". The car went quiet once again.
"Another clue," I said, "the bowler played for a visiting side at Worfield when he was still a school boy."
"That's a great help," said Bill "You had all sorts of teams there when Sir Oliver Leese was president".
"Here we are at the national sports centre," I said, "the quiz question will have to wait until our return journey".
"Now this is the room, and the lads are all under nineteen years of age, so you can see what a wonderful chance for then to develop quick reflexes and improve their game, no matter what the weather is like outside or what time of year it is."

FCCQ Question 66:
Who made the highest individual score in England in 1997?

We watched the game without further conversation. At the end, Bill said "I wish I had had that opportunity when I was as young as them".

"I think Mike Vockins booklet describes the game very well" said Andrew "and I am pleased to see all the players in whites and that it has not developed into a pyjama game yet."

"It is twenty five years since Mike held their first demonstration match here. Now that camcorders have been developed so much, do you not think it would be possible to do an indoor cricket promotional video".

With that thought in mind, we started our drive back to North Wales.

"Now what about this let-arm spinner" said Andrew. " Doug Slade, he played for Shropshire after he finished at Worcestershire, it wasn't him, was it?"
" Good thinking, but no." " Norman Gifford". "No."

"I will give you a further clue" I said "the batsman was the only bowler to take a hat-trick of victims all under the L B W law".

"I know who that was," said both of my passengers in one voice.

"He played for Gloucestershire," said Bill, "But we need to know who they were playing against."

There was another quiet spell, then Bill said "Six consecutive sixes you said". " Yes, that's right," I replied. "But not all in the same over," said Andrew.

FCCQ Question 67:
Who holds the record for the most runs scored in a month, and how many?

"As we are getting close to your house now Bill, I will give you another clue," I said. "The name of the bowler who bowled a maiden over between the four sixes and the first two balls of the next was Ian Botham."

"That means Worcestershire or Somerset," said Bill. "I know who it is now, an interesting thought, I wonder how many captains would have given him another over when the last four balls had cost 24 runs."

"Are you getting out here as well, Andrew?" Yes, but I am not going to bed before I have got this b***** bowlers name," said a frustrated cricket fanatic.

With that final comment, we wished one another goodnight and I left them with the knowledge that Bill knew the answer. Do you?

* * * * *

How many players; names did you spot?

25
50
75
100

or more?

FCCQ Question 68:
How many runs did Graham Gooch score on his Test debut?

INDOOR CRICKET

In 1971, fellow grass roots cricketers in Shropshire started an indoor cricket league. Mike Vokins, now secretary of Worcestershire county cricket club, together with Eddie Rowe and Peter Sellars devised the game that enables the real enthusiast all the year round cricket.

I am delighted to the able to reproduce a full set of the rules as proposed by Mike and his colleagues.

I endorse completely the requirement that players should be properly attired to participate in the game in order that it is taken seriously.

Your attention is drawn to the paragraphs on "local TRANSLATION of rules" and also "ball by ball".

I understand that 25 years later, the league is still being run, which would suggest that the sons of the fathers have taken to all the year round cricket.
It also proves that the three originators of the game must have come up with the right formula. Congratulations to them.

LAWS OF INDOOR SIX-A-SIDE CRICKET

The game was devised to offer cricketers the opportunity to plain cricket during the close season, and every attempts was made to make this six-a-side game as near to the outdoor game [in concept and in law] as is possible in a confined arena. The reception that the game has received from both players and spectators indicates that these objectives have been achieved.

> FCCQ Question 69:
> Who scored the fastest hundred in 1997?

The laws of cricket shall apply, subject to the following exceptions, additions or amendments:

1. Teams shall be composed of six players who shall be properly attired for the game of cricket.

2. Each match shall be of one innings per team, each innings to be a maximum of 12 six ball owners. No bowler shall bold more than four owners in each innings.

3. Two batsman shall be on the field of play at any one time as in the normal game. In the event of the team losing five wickets before completion of its allotted 12 overs. The last man may bat on with the penultimate batsman remaining as a runner.

4. [a] a ball struck to it the wall behind the bowler [boundary wall] without hitting another wall shall be four runs if the ball has hit the ground, or six runs if it hits the boundary wall directly.

[b] a ball struck to hit one or more side or back walls shall be one run, even though the ball may subsequently hit the boundary wall.

[c] if the striker plays the ball with the bat and a run is completed, three runs shall be scored. This applies whether or not the ball has hit a side or back wall, but does not apply to boundary hits.

[d] a bye shall be scored as two runs; a leg-bye shall be one run. In the event of a run being taken on byes or leg-byes, three runs shall be scored for each completed run.

[e] an overthrow hitting any wall shall be one run to the batsman.

FCCQ Question 70:
Who scored the second fastest hundred in 1997?

5. Dismissals:

[a] the striker may be out caught if the ball hit by him is caught by a fielder after it has hit a wall [other than a direct hit onto the boundary wall] or ceiling, providing the ball has not touched the ground.

[b] the last batsman will be given out if the penultimate batsman [running with him] is run out.

6. Result:

The team scoring most runs in its innings shall be the winning team. In the event of the scores being equal the team losing the least member of wickets shall be declared the weather. If the result is still equal the game shall be a tie.

LOCAL TRANSLATION OF THE RULES

Many cricketers will have played cricket on those grounds where a local translation of the laws off the game is employed. This does not refer to the "bending" of the laws by the local umpire [depending on whether the home or visiting side is batting] but to those factors that require the laws to be adjusted slightly. The large chestnut tree within the boundary rope, the ten foot high hedge that constitutes the boundary on a small ground and over which a four most the struck to be scored as six; these are the sort of things that require translation of the laws. We all know grounds where search local laws are used.

Similarly, the laws of indoor cricket apply to ideal arenas, but where local difficulties, windows, doors, wall-bars, beans, etc are encountered, local rules may be incorporated; e.g. a four going behind a wall-bar will be awarded the appropriate score, and the ball immediately deemed to be dead.

Where beams support a roof; it may be agreed to consider the beam or last two beams nearest the boundary wall to be scored as boundaries also. In some arenas, especially very narrow ones, the fielders are close enough to inhibit batsmen running at all, so to further encourage running between wickets a "running crease" approximately two yards from the

FCCQ Question 71:
Who scored the third fastest hundred in 1997?

stumps may be drawn across the wickets.

On taking a run a batsman makes his ground when reaching this crease; if a run is refused or when backing up at the non-strikers end, a batsman must make his ground at the opening crease. In large halls, the "three runs per run" system may be needed to reduce to two [or maybe even one].

Creases are best marked on wooden floors with half-inch wide scotch tape. Wickets of the spring-loaded type are eminently suitable for indoor cricket.

BALL BY BALL

One of the early problems in devising indoor cricket was the difficulty in finding a suitable ball.

In the early years a composition ball, the C 61, by Lilywhite and Froud, proved the most successful. However, the popularity of the indoor game has resulted in a purpose made indoor cricket ball made by Alfred Reader & Co and is available from all good sports shops. There is a choice of colors, red, orange or yellow. This gives you options dependent on the background of the venue as these can vary considerably in multi-purpose halls.

FCCQ Question 72:
Who was the first batsman to score 1000 runs in 1997?

'PLAY'

Indoor cricket was given a good send-of him the winter of 1970-71 when a league competition was formed. This competition provided firm evidence that the game of indoor cricket had match to offer.

It was quite possible that, once the novelty value had worn off; indoor cricket might die a quiet and unmourned death. If; however, it could withstand a fairly extensive examination in a competitive atmosphere then undoubtedly the game was here to stay.

The eight clubs in north west Shropshire, who had been party to the original decision to attempt to device indoor cricket, formed a the in October 1970. For matches were played at Ellesmere college on Tuesday evenings throughout that winter. As each match lasted not more than one are, to matches were played each evening-and the evenings thus had the added benefit of bring together four cricket clubs on a winters night.

The clubs taking part in this first-ever indoor cricket tournament were Alberbury, Bomere Heath, Cae Glas, Ellesmere, Frankton, Oswestry, Whittington and The Commoners [a team comprise of members of Ellesmere College Common Room]. At first, matches tended to be one-sided, but when or clubs had played one game, their awareness of the tactical requirements of indoor cricket increased and all further games were more closely contested.

FCCQ Question 73.
Who topped the batting averages in 1997?

The points system used dealing the competition was:
for a win – 5 points
for a tie – 21/2 points

Additionally, batting and bowling points could be scored which enabled for clubs [even those who lost several matches] to maintain their interest in the competition.

The winners of this the competition were the Commoners.

THE EXPERTS OPINION.

Norman Gifford
"After playing, I came to the conclusion that indoor cricket presents the opportunity for a player to develop his game. It certainly sharpens the running between wickets and also the close in feeling!
"I enjoyed the experience and look forward to playing again, not least as a means of practice with the county".

Basil D'Olivera
Having been converted to the game as an alternative to indoor nets.
"Any time. It's real fun, it has others and it's magnificent for sharpening reactions. You've really got to move."

So there you are, folks, find the right menu and keep in trim all winter. Better than going straight to the pub and it will give you something to talk about when you do get there.

> FCCQ Question 74:
> Who took the most wickets in 1997?

Cricket is a great game for the statistician. Start your own records and then try to break them.

Best Team Score
Lowest Team Score

Best Batting
Best Bowling

Best Fielding
Best Wicket Keeping

Make the game competitive. It's fun and that is what cricket should be all about.

FCCQ Question 75:
Who was the leading wicket keeper in 1997?

THE ANNUAL CRICKET DINNERS

The annual dinner should be one of the main social events of any cricket club. At Worfield we have been fortunate enough to have established a tradition that it is an all male event held on the last Friday in November every year.

The first one I attended was over 40 years ago when about 42 of us squeezed into "Ma's Bar" at the Davenport Arms in the village.

The numbers grew and we held a number of dinners at either The Falcon or The Swan in Bridgnorth. Being out of the parish meant that the various landlords of the Wheel, the Royal Oak, the Cow and the Dog all needed an escort home by the local members.

On one such occasion, we had returned to the Dog where Walter Eccleston was mine host. There were a few of us sat in the tap room drinking Walters health, when a uniformed officer of the law appeared in the doorway. "Allo, 'allo, 'allo, what's going on here?" he said. "I'm just having a few drinks with my friends" slurred Walter.

"A right load of friends you've got" said the local copper. "How much was that last round?" he asked. " Nobody is paying," said Walter. "You awkward old B –" said the constable. "How much would it be if someone had been paying?" "Oh, about 17 shillings and 6 pence," said Walter. "Right! And here is a quid for the next round and mine is a scotch." said the copper who was a bit peeved at having missed the dinner because of extra duties.

> *FCCQ Question 76:*
> *Who was the leading fielder in 1997?*

86

We have been very fortunate to have had a number of speakers from Warwickshire county cricket club over the years. None better than Leslie Deakins, the former club secretary. He could recall stories concerning past cricketers of all counties throughout the country and we were delighted that Leslie was able to speak to us on a number of occasions.

Leslie said a vast selection of the general public were not aware of the many stories that abound from the game of cricket and on one occasion was confronted with the statement that most stories concerned Yorkshire cricket with the majority credited to Freddie Trueman. Leslie replied by saying he could tell at least two stories relating to every first class county and proceeded to do so.

Stories on players like J.E.B.B.P.Q.C. Dwyer, and not just plain "E.B." as he was known and played for Sussex for five years from 1909. He gave him his full name: John Elicius Benedict Bernard Placid Quirk Carrington Dwyer.

Mr Deakins was a one club man, arriving at Warwickshire as a boy and was Secretary from 1944 to 1976. His classic definition of a committee was, "Like a bunch of bananas; they start green, turn yellow and, in the end, there isn't a straight one in the bunch."

One story Leslie told was of "The lesser known Barnes" and, no, that's not a breed of bird. It concerned Billy Barnes of Nottingham, and a character in his own right.

Billy arrived at Lords drunk one day when Middlesex were entertaining Nottingham, if entertaining is the correct

> *FCCQ Question 77:*
> *How many ways is it possible for a runner to cause a batsman for whom he is acting to be given out?*

description, which, somehow, seems doubtful. However, very intoxicated was Billy, but in an attempt to conceal the fact, the captain still sent him in No. 3, and he was very quickly on his way to the crease. He then proceeded to score a hundred in less that two hours.

The skipper still felt it essential to make a full report to Trent Bridge. Barnes was quickly summoned before the committee to be read the riot act. When they had finished, Billy said "Well, your Lordships, Ah can only say Ah'm sorry, right sorry, that Ah am. But, begging your Lordships' pardons, it strikes me as being like this, beggin' your Lordships' pardons. If Ah can go down to Lords, get drunk and mek a century 'fore lunch, then Ah think it ud pay t'Notts Committee to get mi drunk afore every match, beggin' your Lordships' parden of course".

How do you follow that? Perhaps best by going "back to grass roots".

On another occasion, we escorted dear old George Jones back to the Red Cow. At some point in the proceedings, George stood up and said "It's alright for you young blokes, I've had enough. I'm going to bed, you carry on, everything is half a crown. Good night." And off he went.

A pint pot was placed on the bar and a drink was included for George in every round that was bought. George had been gone quite a while when there came a tap on the window. Jack Turner said, "Christ! It's the missus." They only lived next door; that broke up the party.
The next day we went down to the recreation room to help prepare the room for a Christmas bazaar and I met my pal Edwin Golden who had gone to the Royal Oak on the previous night. "How did you finish up last night?" Said Edwin. "Oh!" I said, "George went to bed and everything was going fine until Jack Turner's missus tapped the window, and Jack said "Christ, it's the missus!" and that was 4 o' clock. Whereupon I

FCCQ Question 78:
What is the highest number of catches in an innings in the Benson & Hedges Cup and who held them?

88

received a tap on the shoulder and turned round and an irate lady said "It was Jack's missus and it was 5 o' clock."

M J K Smith was also our guest speaker on a couple of occasions. When you recall the side he skippered which was reported to the one of the happiest bunch of cricketers to tour, you can imagine he had a number of anecdotes to tell.

However, none of them come to mind and they would, no doubt, have already be recorded in print. Here are two that you will not have heard before.

At Worfield we have an outstanding list of vice presidents and these two stories relate to two sadly deceased members.

Lady Foster last year celebrated her 100th birthday thus becoming a centurion of a different kind. In order to receive the customary congratulations from the queen, it is necessary to produce a birth certificate.

As she had only recently taken up residence in a local nursing home, her son was having difficulty in locating the papers. However, when he visited her one day, she took a box out of a drawer and passed it across to her son with a twinkle in her eye

FCCQ Question 79:
What is the highest 10th wicket partnership in the Benson & Hedges Cup?

"When were you born, John?" When he told her she then handed him her birth and wedding certificates and said " I think you will find that that makes you legitimate then."

The Prebendary Thompson O.B.E., a past president of the club, attended his last there on his 95th birthday. The porch to the village church had been plagued with pigeons making an awful mess in the main entrance to the church. One morning, the local sexton was just coming out of the church shouting "Shoo, b***** off" just as the vicar came round the corner and admonished him saying "Now, now, Will, there is no need for that. All you have to do is say Shoo! and they will B***** off'.

The Bible states that creation is not consistent with the evolution theory that man is descended from a monkey. Eve made a monkey out of Adam. Eve started our sex with a forbidden fruit complex and all with have had it ever since. If that apple in the Garden of Eden had not be forbidden, Eve would never have noticed it.

When some big PRUNE
The son of a NUT
Marries a LEMON
And the PEAR
Have a PEACH
For a daughter
With CHERRY lips
And ROSES in her cheeks
How in the Devil
Can you believe in Heredity?

> *FCCQ Question 80:*
> *What are the maximum length and width, in inches, of a cricket bat?*

As stated in the introduction to this book, I was inspired by Brian Johnston. That cricket, and in fact life, should be fun I would like to say how much Test Match Special can be enjoyed even when there is no play. The beauty of cricket is that there is never a shortage of opinion on prospects of the game and to listen to old players recalling matches of their day makes for fascinating listening.

I do not know whether Tony Lewis is a fishermen or not, but I doubt if his arms would be long enough to describe the one that got away. This assumption is made on hearing his description of a delivery that dismissed him that was bowled by Roly Jenkins he said, "I was out in Worcester to a ball that pitched in Herefordshire.

The fact that fielders complained of having to retrieve the ball from the neighboring county when Jessop was batting seems more feasible.

Village cricket envelopes every aspect of life. Nature, travel, facts of life, drink etc and here are stories that touch on all those things.

It is said that if you want to find a fool in the country take him with you. Nipper Cook was a renowned poacher in south Shropshire. One day when he was helping himself to some fine trout out of the river that flowed through the local estate, he was somewhat surprised by the local squire.

"Got you, Cook!" said the squire. "However, seeing that it is the first time I have managed to catch you, I will let you off;

FCCQ Question 81:
If the ball is hit by a batsman direct onto a protective helmet worn by a short leg fieldsman and is caught by another fielder without the ball touching the ground, is the batsman out?

but do not let me catch you fishing these waters again or you will be in trouble. " Very good sir," said Nipper touching his forelock.

About a week later, Nipper, who must have being losing his touch, was caught once more. " Caught you again, Cook," said the squire. "I thought I told you not to let me catch you fishing these waters again." "Oh no sir," said Nipper, "Those waters you woo talking about must be past Bristol by now."

Chimney sweeps are also characters, and it must be a thirsty job. Anyway, after a hard days work, the local chimney sweep spent the last few hours at the pub, soot covered face and all. When he left plaiting his feet, he took a short cut through the churchyard and succeeded in falling into a newly dug grave where he slept of the effect of the local brew.

In the early hours of the next morning, the postman was also using the same short cut and as he passed the new grave, a black face poked up out of the ground and said, "What time is it?" It is said that the letters were delivered very early that morning.

A

Very Early Delivery

FCCQ Question 82:
If there is a boundary fence, is the bowler allowed to lean against it or over it to take a catch?

Dave Allen tells another story with regard to a drunk falling down an open grave, trying to get out and finally sleeping it off; only to be rudely awakened by another fellow falling on top of him. The first occupant woke up and said" You'll not get out of here." But he did!

On a trip to London by rail, there were four gents in civilian clothing, all strangers to one another and one opened the conversation. "It looks as if we are stuck with one another's company for the next few hours." He said. "I suggest we introduce ourselves to start with. Although I am traveling in mufty, I am a Brigadier, married with three sons, all engineers." "Ah!" said a second man, "I too am a Brigadier, married with three sons, all doctors." "How extraordinary" said a third, "I, too, an a Brigadier, married with three sons, all lawyers." Whereupon all three turned on the fourth man. "Sorry to disappointment you, gents" he said, "I am a private, not married, but I have three sons, all Brigadiers."

At Speakers Corner in Hyde Park, a man got up on the soap box and said "I want to speak about the evils of drink and to demonstrate this evil I will give you an illustration." He then held up two glasses, both with a clear liquid in them. " In this glass is water, dear old H 2 0, and in this glass, neat gin." He then proceeded to drop a worm into the water and the worm wriggled about. He then dropped a worm into the gin and it went straight to the bottom of the glass and laid straight out as stiff as a board. "Which just goes to prove" he said... But before he could get another word out, a wag at the black of the crowd shouted out "If you've got worms, drink gin."

FCCQ Question 83:
Which player scored the highest aggregate number of runs in the 1997 season?

Moving on to the next speaker, there was a lady extolling the virtues of love and marriage. As an example she was referring to a celebrity of the time who's wife had just given birth to their second child. "Now there was a man," she said, "A man who made love with his eyes." Once again, the wag from the back shouts up "He must have been cock-eyed then."

These stories endorse the social side of grass roots cricket Obviously, speakers talk about the achievements of the club and the highs and lows of the season, but these would be of little interest to Joe Public.

A number of insurance companies combined forces and recruited the services of an artist to design a crest for the new company. He produced his design and presented to a meeting of the company directors. The sketch of a shield divided into four with a circle in the middle. In each corner of the shield there was a drawing of a couple in a double bed, and in the circle, a baby in a cradle.

"Whilst we admire your draughsmanship" they said, "perhaps you would like to explain the contents of your design".
Certainly" he said, "quite simple, in the first bed we have a husband and wife representing Legal and General. In the second bed, an engaged couple – Mutual Trust. In the third bed, a prostitute and a customer - Commercial Union. While in the fourth bed is a boss and his secretary, representing Employers Liability."
"Very good so far," the directors said, "but what about this baby in the cradle?" – "Oh! General Accident!"

FCCQ Question 84:
Which batsman made the highest individual score in 1997 and what was it?

Two business associates were playing golf one day, and as they were both good golfers, they were making good progress when they came up behind two ladies who were having trouble getting round. "Why don't you go and see if they will let us play through?" said one of the men to the other. Off he went and suddenly came running back. "Perhaps you would like to go," he said, "You see it is a bit embarrassing as one is my wife and the other is my mistress". "0. K." said the other, and off he went. A few minutes later he was back. "Well how did you get on?" said his partner. "Small world, isn't it?" was the reply.

Talking of golf clubs, there was a time I shared an office with a fellow called Tony who was a member of the local golf club. He came in one Monday morning and was telling Beth, our secretary and me about the wife swapping and handy panky that out been going on at his club that weekend. "I cannot be doing with it," he said, "I would rather have a good steak these days". Well, a few days later, a very smart and beautiful mini-skirted young lady, a real stunner, walked into our office. Tony's eyes nearly popped out of his head. Beaming all over his face "Can I help you?" he said, and they got into conversation. When the young lady finally left the room with Tony still drooling, Beth leant across the desk and asked "Gone off steak, Tony?"

Another of our vice presidents, John Pigg, is, naturally enough with a name like that, a farmer. There was a city gent with an open top sports car driving along one day when he had to slow down to avoid the animals on the road. A little further on, he spotted the village policeman, and shouted across "There are some cattle out by the crossroads". "Oh! them'll be Pigg's,"

FCCQ Question 85:
How many fielders took 20 or more catches in the 1997 season?

said the local copper. "No, the're b***** cows, I do know the difference" said the irate driver, driving off never knowing what the policeman meant.

When Noah built the Ark, he found a hole in the bottom of the boat so he placed the dog's nose in the hole until he fixed the leak, and that is why a dog's nose is always cold. Then he placed his wife's feet over the hole, and that is why women have cold feet. Then he sat on the hole, and that is why men always stand with their backs to the fire.

There was a Canon who had three sons, two of them were also clergymen, while the third might be described as the prodigal son.

One morning, the Canon was standing in front of the fire, airing his knowledge, when the eldest son came into the room. "Good morning, father", "Good morning, son. Did you have a good night?" "Marvellous night, dreamt of heaven". "Oh, yes, and what was that like, son?" "Just like home, father, just like home". He then went and stood alongside his father, both with their backs to the fire.

A few minutes later, the second son, complete with dog collar, came in and they all exchanged "Good morning" greetings and the father asked "Did you have a good night, son?" "Wonderful night, father, dreamt of heaven". "Oh, indeed, and what was that like?" "Just like home, father, just like home". He then went and stood on the other side of his father, all three with their backs to the fire.

Sometime later, the third son came in, yawning his head off.

FCCQ Question 86:
A N Aymes made 7 stumpings for Hants in the 1997 season. Who was the only other keeper to equal that number?

Again, they all exchanged "Good morning" greetings and the father asked the same question. "Did you have a good night, son?" "Very good night, thank you, father." "Did you have a dream?" "Yes, I did, father, I dreamt of Hell". "Is that so, and what is it like?"

A Warm Future

"Just like home, father, just like home; couldn't see the fire for ruddy parsons."

The dinners also have a serious side, like the cost of playing today, but I expect it is pro rata --- my first bat cost £5 over forty years ago -- I suppose the equivalent today would cost about £200.

Whilst on a serious note, I would like to refer to that wonderful writer Neville Cardus, whose formal education finished at the age of thirteen. Whilst writing about Wilfred Rhodes note that there is no mention of spin or speed in a paragraph he described as the best piece of prose of his life.

FCCQ Question 87:
Who was the player to take a wicket with the first ball of his first class career in 1997?

"Flight was his secret, flight and the curving line, now higher, now lower, tempting, inimical, every ball like every other ball, yet somehow, unlike, each over in collusion with the others, part of a plot. Every ball a decoy, a spy sent out to get the lie of the land; some balls simple, some complex, some easy, some difficult; and one of them – ah, which? – the master ball."

The expert art of one man describing the expert art of another.

Talking of experts, John Arlott was the expert commentator who gave pleasure to millions and I cannot let the opportunity pass without referring to one of his little gems. In a match in which Clive Rice and Paddy Clift were playing together, he said "It had to happen, Rice bowls and Paddy fields."

I always admire a person who can tell a story against themselves. Arthur Mailey told the story of how he was attending a dinner dance one evening and was asked by the lady hostess if he would be dancing later, to which he replied "I think not, I'm a little stiff from bowling". "Oh! that's where you come from," retorted the dowager lady.

The attitude of Les Ames appeals to me when he was caught in the deep off Tom Goddard. "Well, I'd rather be caught there than at short leg".

There is food for thought from W.G. when he said "I hate defensive strokes, you can only get three off 'em." He also said something that is as true today as in his day: "Games aren't won by leaving the ball alone."

Patsy Hendren was a very wise man. When asked why he had decided to retire, he said, "While you can still ask why rather than when."

FCCQ Question 88:
How many players finished with a batting average of over fifty in the 1997 season?

Let me finish this chapter with a story concerning my schoolboy hero, Denis Compton. He was in the middle of one of his many long innings for Middlesex and, during the tea break, Walter Robins said "Denis, I have never seen you hit a straight six" to which my hero replied "Watch the third ball after tea". Walter watched and, sure enough, Denis took two steps down the wicket and the ball sailed over the sight screen. "Pure genius," said Walter, "Pure genius".

Sorry, the last word should go to our grassroots representative at cricket headquarters.

David Knowles, the son of the headmaster I referred to on the first page and with whom I started school some sixty years ago, is now one of the official guides to various parties visiting Lords.

He was approached by a young fellow who wanted to know whether it would be possible for him to propose marriage to his girlfriend in the gardens. David had to tell him he was sorry that would not be possible that day as they were filming some form of documentary there, but added he was sure there would be some opportune moment during the tour that he would be able to pop the question. Sure enough, while they were in the long room, the young man went down on one knee and made his proposal to a spontaneous round of applause from the other members of the party. David reckons that, to his knowledge, he is the only fellow who can claim to have bowled a maiden over in the long room at Lords.

FCCQ Question 89:
How many players that played in the First Test for England in 1998 finished in the top 20 batsmen in the 1997 averages?

THE GHOST OF DAVENPORT PARK

The old cricket pavilion has gone now, but have the mysteries that surrounded it gone too?

Have the players of today experienced the same, inexplicable, phenomena that their fathers and grandfathers did in the nineteen sixties?

Remember, there was no bar or hard liquour on the ground in those days, as, no doubt, that would have been put forward as the reason for "seeing things" as, indeed, it would today.

However, I pose the question: Has anyone been waiting at the ground for a friend, believing themselves to be all alone?

On a warm Summer's evening, as the sun sets in the west, a rabbit scurries into the hedgerow, a black cat jumps on top of the wall, its green eyes flashing as it searches its prey.

It is deadly quiet, the daylight has suddenly gone and the nocturnal wildlife is springing to life all around you. You are expecting your friend to come from one direction, yet you have the uneasy feeling that you are being watched from another.

Would anyone who has experienced such a sensation go on oath and deny the presence of a third party?

FCCQ Question 90:
How many players were used by England and by Australia in the whole 1997 series?

Did the mysterious happenings of the sixties disappear forever with the removal of the old pavilion, or did the ghost ride away on the old Ransome when it was sold? Is he, whoever he, or it, was, just lying dormant, waiting to haunt the next generation of cricketers as they relax and become complacent in the comfort of their new clubhouse? Will he or it return to exercise the Freedom of Davenport Park" as occurred thirty odd years ago?

Adolph, as his name was whispered, was a spasmodic summer phantom that "appeared" around the pavilion of Worfield Cricket Club. It is strange how he only seemed to appear after teams from the Black Country had been visiting. Sides coming from the rural depths of Shropshire never seemed to incur his wrath. However, after Goodyear, Hobsons or other

FCCQ Question 91:
How many players played in all six tests in 1997 for both England and Australia?

101

works sides from Wolverhampton had been the opponents, the guttural sounds could be heard and the shadowy movements noticed behind the pavilion and toilet block.

He was christened Adolph because Old Ben reckoned it was one of the German prisoners of war that did not understand cricket and didn't like townies either.

We had been at the ground at various times of the day and night throughout the year, but he had never been "seen" or "heard" in the winter, only in the cricket season.

There were a few locals at the time who believed he was not nearly so active after the China Bridge was taken down, cutting off direct access from the park to the church because he was unable to get spiritual guidance any more.

Some said he wintered in the Dovecot and because of this no longer used the short cut through the park to Davenport Hall. According to Old Bish he was sure he hibernated in The Old Ice House on the way down to Mervyn Tucker's at Mere Pool.

Yet the Summer when he was most active was following the cold winter of 1963 when we moved two old timber pavilions from the RAF Camp at Stanmore. The material was then used to build an implement shed to house the tractor and motor mowers.

Ray Roberts was of the opinion that Adolph was a bilingual squadron leader we had upset by moving their pavilions.

FCCQ Question 92:
How many centuries were scored by England and by Australia in the 1997 series?

It was always at a full moon, where the moonlight shone across the park casting irregular shadows across the cricket ground from the dead trees in the park. There would be an uneasy calm with only a handful of players left in the pavilion before adjourning to "The Dog". There would be this noise, "Ach Tung, Ach Tung". The players nearest the door would rush outside, but always too late, just shadows disappearing behind the new implement shed. They would come back in and finish packing their cricket gear, still not knowing what had caused that very distinctive sound.

We would go outside, stop and listen and watch, but nothing. We then made sure everything was looked up and went down to the pub, as we all felt in need of a drink. Not a word to the landlord or he would have sworn we had been drinking elsewhere beforehand.

FCCQ Question 93:
How many times did a bowler take 5 wickets in an innings for Australia in the 1997 series?

Should Adolph return, the youngsters of today will no doubt think that it is a Klingon, as it was very much the sound of a robot come to think of it, the sixties was a prime time for UFOs.

Ray and I had been picking mushrooms one moonlit night, they glow silver in that light and a cricket cap full is an ideal amount for breakfast with home cured bacon and egg. Oh! the delights of country life.

Well, I had left my scooter at the cricket ground so Ray dropped me off from his car at about midnight. " Watch out for the squadron leader," said Ray. " Good night, Ray" I said. "Goodnight Ed, Goodnight, Adolph" was the reply. I was just fastening on my crash helmet and I heard this eerie sound.
"Oh my god, it's him", I thought. Then I listened again. It was a trumpet being played, ye gods, he's joined forces with Gabriel. I paused a minute and then recognised it as "the Last Post" getting a bit morbid now, I thought. "Ach Tung" I said to myself as I started up my scooter and went home for a good night's sleep to be followed by a nice Sunday breakfast.

We were playing The Express and Star that day and when I arrived at the ground, Ray said "Hello, Ed, have any company last night". " No just accompaniment" I replied. " Oh, you heard Gus Hickman as well, did you Eddie,"said Jeff. " He's practicing for Remembrance Day. He's playing because we can't have the RAF band anymore". "Has he played any German music yet" said Ray. "That would prove very interesting," chorused Roy and Dave who had just entered the room.

FCCQ Question 94:
How many stumpings were made for England andfor Australia in the 1997 series?

"It's a full moon tonight lads," said a familiar figure in the doorway. "Ach tung, Meine Furher," said Bish as Henry, the captain, appeared. "At ease men," said Henry.

The Bridgnorth Journal had been running a series concerning "Old Mo" – he was supposed to be a ghost that haunted The Old Friary along by the river Severn in Bridgnorth, so ghosts were flavor of the month.

"Not a word to this lot about Adolph," said Ben" or the report will be all about ghosts and nothing about cricket". We did not know what to expect from Adolph that right as Express and Star were from Wolverhampton but could not be described as a works side. Would he pay us a visit or not?

We enjoyed a very good game that ended in a draw with honours about even. There was one appeal for a catch behind the wicket, but John Clark turned it down. But as Bish said, "he'd never seen or heard Adolph either." "I definitely heard something," claimed Roy, "I saw it move off the bat" said Dave the bowler. "You two had better come mushrooming with me and Ed after" said Ray, "then perhaps you might see or hear the squadron leader."

Having enjoyed a very sociable evening with the men of the press at The Davenport Arms, we went on our fungi expedition. All those years ago, the church bells were not being rung because repairs were needed to the steeple, and the clock was supposed to have been silenced. However, just as the four of us returned to the ground, it all started to happen.

> FCCQ Question 95:
> How many players averaged over 50 for the 1997 series for England and Australia and name them.

A police car came screaming up past the gamekeeper's cottage, round by the Blacksmith's shop and down China Bridge Bank. Gus struck up on his trumpet and the church clock stuck twelve. Then at that midnight hour, everything went quiet. We were all out off the car by then, but we froze in our tracks, we were all looking in the direction of the pavilion.

As we stood like statues, a long shadow emerged from behind the building. First a brace of rabbits, although we were not to know at that time, this was followed by a much bigger shadow. Then, in a high pitched male voice, "Ach Tung. Ach Tung" followed, this time, by a deep belly laugh as a figure in an army Great Coat came into view.
"You old b*****, Tommy!" said Roy.

It was Tom Welsby with a couple of rabbits on a stick slung over his shoulder. He had just come from spending a right with his mate Mervyn and was taken a short cut home. " Had a good night lads," he said.
"Goodnight, Goodnight Adolph," and off he went into the night still laughing.

Feeling rather let down, the four of us erstwhile ghost busters bade one another goodnight and went our respective ways home.

When we met at the ground in mid week, the four of us were met by a bunch of grinning cricketers, all enjoying a laugh at our expense, and with logical explanations for all the other happenings on that Sunday night.

FCCQ Question 96:
What milestone did Shane Warne become the ninth Australian to reach during the first innings of the final test in 1997?

Apparently there had been an accident at just before twelve o' clock, hence the screaming police car. The verger had forgotten about the repairs to the steeple and wound the church clock by mistake. Whereas Mrs. Hickman would not let Gus practice his trumpet until she had finished watching her favorite film on television.

"But what about Adolph?" said a late corner onto the scene.
"What Adolph?" we all said. "The spook, of course," he said. "Sorry, but there is no spook. It was Tom Welsby."

"Ah! here's Marcus," said Ben, "That was typical of your uncle Torn, Marcus" he said. "Yea, he enjoyed himself on Sunday night" said Marcus, "But I'll tell you something else; he's been in hospital the last three months, and only came out last Wednesday."

FCCQ Question 97.
Who topped the bowling averages in 1997?

WOODCOCK'S HUNDRED

The list as featured on page 27 of WISDEN '98 is as stated "Inevitably invidious and essentially provocative," so let's start the arguments.

I oan find little on Alfred Mynn except that he was "A Giant"
W. Bedlam, J. Srnail, A.G .Steel and A Shaw may well be worthy of selection but I have no knowledge of their achievements.

There are, however, some very strong contenders for inclusion, but in what order of merit and at the exclusion of which players on the existing list, I throw open to debate.

To justify inclusion on a list of the "100 greatest cricketers of all time," a player must surely have produced statistics to warrant his selection.

What better than – 100 Hundreds –
12 of these are missing:
E.H. Hendren, C.P. Mead, T.W. Graveney, Zaheer Abbas,
T.W. Hayward, JET Edrich, A. Sandham, G.M. Turner, L.E.G. Ames, G.E. Tyldesley, D.L. Amiss and G.A. Hick.

P.G.H. Fender (Fastest Hundred)

R.J. Shastri (Fastest Double Hundred and 6 Sixes in one over)

A.E. Fagg (Two Double Hundreds in a Match)

In the list we have a number of players listed yet their playing partners are not.

FCCQ Question 98:
How many bowlers that played in the First Test for England in
1998 finished in the top twenty of the 1997 bowling averages?

Wes Hall is listed but Charlie Griffith is not.
D.K. Lillee is listed but Jeff Thompson is not.
Jim Laker but no Tony Lock
C.E.L. Ambrose but no CA Walsh
S. Ramadin but no A. Valentine

The biggest omission of all must be A.P. Freeman, the second greatest wicket taker of all time; all ten wickets three times and 304 wickets in a season.

What about 16 wickets in a Test by N.D. Hirwani and R.A.L. Massie
Or
15 wickets in a Test by J. Briggs, C. Blythe or H. Verity.

Rodney Marsh with 355 dismissals in Tests stakes a claim for the wicket keepers.

Remember when the West Indies had a battery of four fast bowlers There is no mention of "Big Bird" Joel Garner.

While these fast bowlers blew away the opposition who scored the runs and put them on the road to success, remember the two opening bats who both played over 100 times for their country. That's right, Desmond Haynes and Gordon Greenidge.

I note that ten players playing today are listed, but that does not include an English man who has captained his country in over fifty Test Matches and was recently named man of the series in England's win over South Africa – Michael Atherton.

FCCQ Question 99:
What is the highest individual score made in the Benson &
Hedges Cup and who made it?

Four former England captains also come to mind: M.J.K. Smith, R. Illingworth, A.W. Grieg and M.W. Gatting. Don't forget Alex Stewart, not many players have scored two centuries in the same Test Match

Muttiah Muralitharan and maybe Jayasuriva and P. de Silva stake a claim on behalf of Sri Lanka

I find it difficult to name the top 100 English players without the obvious claims of the odd Aussie or one or two West Indians, Kiwi or other of the Test playing nations.

The question remains which country would claim to have produced the greatest number of players in the "100 Greatest Cricketers of all Time"?

Can anyone add to this list and then put them in order of merit. Perhaps John Woodcock would like to revise his list.

Should the player referred to in the question below also be listed in the "100 Greatest"?

FCCQ Question 100:
Most bowlers today would be happy with an average of about 20 runs per Test wicket. What average did Lohman achieve in taking 112 Test Wickets?

FIRST CLASS FUTURE – A GRASSROOTS BLUEPRINT

So Lord McLaurin's proposals have been rejected by the first class counties. That will have come as no surprise considering the clubs voting on the issues. All the clubs in the lower half of the championship table would be voting to retain their first class status.

If any progress is to be made, the involvement of clubs outside the first class game needs to be given a vote.

This is my "Grassroots Blueprint for the advancement of cricket nationwide".

There are 40 clubs playing first class and minor counties cricket including Oxford and Cambridge universities.

There is an obvious need for a more competitive format to be introduced throughout the game in order to stimulate the players and watching public alike.

Finance is the great issue here, for any club to survive, they must look at what they have to sell and the market in which a are operating. Sponsorship has been a great boost, but will only continue to help the clubs who help themselves. If public interest is not maintained and developed to the satisfaction of the sponsors, this support will disappear.

To improve the competitive edge, it is essential to create a promotion and relegation system with a number of divisions.

FCCQ Question 101:
Name the English bowler who is the only player to take 10 wickets in the West Indies.

The problem at the moment is that clubs involved are too close to the situation to be objective and "can't see the wood for the trees". Every other cricket lover up and down the country sees the need for change. Whereas the clubs voting on the issue are all" stuck in the mud" and afraid that it might be their club that is relegated.

That might be the best thing that could happen to them. Being top of division two and fighting for promotion would have far more public appeal than floundering at the bottom of an outdated championship table as at present. My " grassroots blueprint" is for four divisions, each often clubs.

The first two divisions to play the other nine clubs in their division, both at home and away, a total of eighteen four day matches.

Division 3 to play eighteen three day matches. Division 4 to play eighteen two day matches. Division 1 and 2 to combined in a one day Sunday league competition.

The top 10 clubs to twin with division three in order to benefit from any home grown talent in that club, and stimulate interest in both areas.

Division 2 clubs to twin with clubs in division 4 on a similar basis.

There would be promotion and relegation between the division of one club, and an opportunity for a new club to an entry to the fourth division at the expense of the bottom placed club.

FCCQ Question 102:
Name the only West Indian batsman to score over 100 centuries.

A new" F A cup style" competition of 64 teams be introduced, comprising of the 40 aforementioned clubs plus 24 from the winners of various leagues such as Birmingham, Bradford, Lancashire and so on.

This would create an opportunity for the little clubs to play against the top sides in the country, would be a money spinner for them and produce the odd shock result has so often happens in the football world.

A competition such as this under the control of the national cricket association would help foster better relationships between the various grades of cricket. I am sure a sponsor could be found for such an event, the name of "Littlewoods" comes to mind.

My personal preference would be to make it a condition that only players eligible for selection for England could play in this competition, has the object of the exercise is to raise the standard of play in our own players and not further the cause of overseas players.

I invite other grassroots cricketers views on these proposals.

I do not believe " cricket will die in the next 10 years". This statement has been made every decade that I can remember, but I do believe that every so often a new challenge and fresh incentive is required.

It is understood that the Nat West final will be played a week earlier next year. This will have no significant effect in that there will only be 11 minutes difference in the time of sunrise.

FCCQ Question 103:
A batsman can be given out caught if the ball lodges in the
wicket keeper's pads, but would he be given out if it lodged in the grill of
a fielder's protective helmet?

The concern is obviously with regard to how the wicket plays, and the effect of the early morning dew in the first half-hour or more.

There is an alternative in this modern day, why not have an artificial wicket on one side of the square and play on that. It would test the bowlers' ability and also create a short boundary on one side for the batsman to exploit, and fielding sides to defend, and spectators to enjoy.

Better ask Derek Underwood what he thinks. He opened the artificial wicket that was laid at Worfield and very good it is too.

FCCQ Question 104:
Which batsman is out if the non-striker obstructs a fielder attempting to take a catch?

A FIRST CLASS FAMILY BUSINESS

Like many other walks of life, Sons follow their fathers into the family business. This is true today in the game of first class cricket.

Here are some interesting questions concerning first class cricket families a few seasons ago.

1). How many former test cricketers have sons who were registered to play first class county cricket in 1997, not forgetting overseas players.
[1 point for each father and one point for each son named].

2). How many pairs of brothers were registered for 1997 [1 point for each brother named].

3). Name the county which has two pairs of brothers registered with them

4). Name the father and brother of a current player who were both former England captains.

5). Name the three consecutive generations of test cricketers in one family

6). One of the players referred to in question 1 has an uncle on the panel of first class umpires. Name the uncle.

7). Name the former county player whose son played in the 1997 Ashes Tests

8). Name the other former county players and their sons that were registered for the 1997 season.

IT'S AS EASY AS ABC

Can you list this side in alphabetical order?

They all have one thing in common except No. 7

He is Indian, a sort of cad, and a little bit backward.

The first two are Aussies

No.1 is rather wooden

No.2 is nearly 100% batsman

No.3 is most definitely not the least bit feminine

No.4 has made a record score in youth tests

It's "a give-away" at No. 5

"I'm alright" says No. 6

No.8 sounds a bit Irish to me, but I don't know if he be

It's hot and sticky being a wicket-keeper at No. 9

It's no lie what they say about No. 10

The last man may need a little stratagem

(Please note, this side is not listed in batting order)

GRASSROOTS SYSTEM FOR SCORING CHAMPIONSHIP MATCHES

The emphasis of this system is that winning should have more reward than acquiring bonus points and that the extent of the margin should dictate the points awarded.

An innings is the greatest margin obtainable and this would be rewarded with the maximum of 25 points. After, points would be shared between the winners and as follows:

Win by 250 runs or more or 10 wickets 20 points loser 0 points

"	"	200	"	"	9	"	19	"	"	1	"
"	"	175	"	"	8	"	18	"	"	2	"
"	"	150	"	"	7	"	17	"	"	3	"
"	"	125	"	"	6	"	16	"	"	4	"
"	"	100	"	"	5	"	15	"	"	5	"
"	"	75	"	"	4	"	14	"	"	6	"
"	"	50	"	"	3	"	13	"	"	7	"
"	"	25	"	"	2	"	12	"	"	8	"
"	"	1	"	"	1	"	11	"	"	9	"

In the event of a tie, each side would be awarded 10 points. In the event of a draw, each side would be awarded 5 points.

I believe this points system would demand more positive cricket as the only bonus points to be won are when a victory by the margin of one innings is achieved.

No matter what level of cricket is being played, it needs to be competitive to be enjoyable for players and spectators alike and, if there is no enjoyment, why bother?

THE 'ESSENTIAL' GRASSROOTS UMPIRE

Cricket as a way of life
is much better with a wife
When out for a duck
they will say "Bad luck"
but, if it is first ball,
nothing's said at all

They know just when to speak
and when your view to seek.
"Did you get a touch?
Yes, I thought as much".
"That umpire's always the same,
dodgy decisions every game".

When he stands, they're bound to win,
why do you think they buy his gin?"
"When it's theit turn to bat,
don't just ask him Howzat?"
"Say, what do you drink these days?"
and his finger he's sure to raise.

"It's from what they tell me,
he can't help it you see."
"The thought of a few beers,
hand raised, he'll say cheers!"
That provided food for thought,
an umpire who could be bought.

FCCQ Question 105:
The ball becomes dead after "over" is called, would the
umpire have to consider any appeal after this?

So, just when all seemed lost,
and we started to count the cost.
Just to keep him in drink,
and how much could he sink.
Really, what was it worth
to maintain his rotund girth?

Then, the wickets began to fall,
we didn't need his help at all.
On our umpire you could depend,
and, of course, he was the other end.
They couldn't tempt him with a beer, well,
for one thing, he couldn't hear.

Last man out and we had won,
justice had at least been done.
"Ump, did he really take that catch?"
"Well it said so by my watch"
"It's our job to see fair play,
and that ends proceedings for the day".

FCCQ Question 106:
Provided the batsman has not left the playing area, what action
should the umpire take if the captain of the fielding side withdraws an
appeal?

119

WEST INDIES POST MORTEM – 1998 TOUR

Nothing happened in the West Indies to change my mind on team selection. In fact, it only strengthened my belief in the need for a balanced side.

The selectors always seem to think it is important to have that extra batsmen in order to score more runs than the opposing side, whereas, I believe it is essential to have five varied bowlers in order to dismiss the opposition for less than your batsmen score, no matter what the conditions are.

With a balanced side there is no need for a crystal ball to predict how the pitch is going to play, whatever happens your side will be equipped to deal with it.

I was very impressed with Brian Lara's captaincy. He was prepared to try something different, after all, what is the worst thing that can happen. Six sixes in an over. Well it has happened twice, but not in a test match.

Lara held the most catches with 13 which was one more than our wicket keeper Jack Russell. However, Thorpe provided Jack good support with 9 catches.

Each side produced three century makers. England had the highest run scorer in Alec Stewart with 452 runs, but the West Indies had the highest wicket taker in Curtley Ambrose with 30 wickets.

FCCQ Question 107:
Provided there are no more than two fielders on the on side behind the line of the popping crease and the bowler has delivered a fair delivery, what other reason could an umpire have for calling "No ball"?

Dean Hedley took 19 wickets but, in doing so, bowled 61 no balls, a huge factor in conceding 546 runs, a basic fault which must be corrected before he is allowed onto the test arena again.

Tuffnell had to bowl defensively too long and, with it, lost the art of tempting the batsman into mistakes. The main aim of a bowler should be to take wickets not just to restrict the batsman to score runs.

Robert Croft showed a bit more guile and managed to take six wickets in the only test he played.

Mark Ramprakash scored a maiden test century followed by a duck in the next match. A hell of a game cricket.

Remember, whenever there is a great bowling performance, there will be some batting failures and when centuries abound, some poor bowler suffers. It is a case of making the most of every chance that comes your way.

Grassroots cricket was fun and I believe still is. The first class cricketers of the Miller and Compton era also got full enjoyment from the game. I am not sure the current first class players do, to the same degree. I hope they do, but" media pressure" does make it difficult.

What terrible jargon that is "media pressure".

One of my fervent grassroots beliefs is that cricket must be fair!

FCCQ Question 108:
If all the stumps are out of the ground, what must the fielding side do in order to secure a run out?

This is where I think that the powers that be have got it wrong again, and that the so-called first test should be deleted from the records.

The match should be declared " void" and not labeled as a draw.

Firstly, it is not fair to the batsmen who lost their wickets on a pitch that was declared unfit for play.

Secondly, it is not fair that the wickets are credited to bowlers allowed to bowl on a wicket unfit for play.

Finally the game did not take place because the playing surface was unfit and could not proceed even though the weather and light conditions were good. **THAT IS NOT CRICKET.**

FCCQ Question 109:
If both batsmen are called "One short" in attempting a second run, how many runs shall be deducted?

WHAT'S THE SCORE?

Normally, when someone asks, "What's the score" the answer is so many runs for so many wickets, or vice versa if you are an Aussie.

Today, scoring techniques and the accumulation of statistics has introduced a new dimension to the game. Did you know it is possible that you can have a "Ball delivered" but not as a "Ball received", if it is a wide ball, that is. That is official

There is an official textbook of the association of Crickct Umpires and Scorers containing the M.C.C. official laws of cricket with interpretations and definitions for umpires, scorers, players and spectators.

On reading the book, I came across a detail that I was not happy with, so I wrote the following letter to the association, to which I received a very courteous reply:

Dear Sirs

I have a copy of the latest Fully Revised Edition of Tom Smith's excellent book Cricket Umpiring and Scoring.

There is an issue that I would like to take up with you concerning Part 111 Scoring.

It is my opinion that unless the umpire has signaled "Dead Ball" the ball is in play and as such should be counted as a ball either as a legitimate ball, a No Ball or a Wide. Figure Bowling analysis shows:

FCCQ Question 110.
Name the only South African bowler to take a Hat-trick in a Test Match

---

1. J White as bowling 6 full overs plus 1 No Ball & 1 Wide = 38 balls bowled

2. T Brown as bowling 7 full overs plus 1 No Ball = 43 balls bowled

3. M Green as bowling 6.4 overs plus 1 Wide = 41 Bails bowled

4. F Black as bowling 5 full overs plus 1 No Ball = 31 bails bowled

This provides a total of 153 bails bowled in the complete innings.

I agree with this figure and cannot understand why the 2 Wides bowled should be deducted to reduce the number of bails bowled to 151. Particularly when you consider that these two deliveries will have added two runs in the form of extras to the total.

Figure 10 Batting sheet shows:

1. T Stokes 20 balls received whereas he received 21 including a Wide
2. P Morris 3 balls received whereas he received 4 including a Wide which he was given out off stumped

FCCQ Question 111:
Name the only South African bowler to take 200 Test Match wickets.

Had Morris been given out stumped off a Wide first ball he faced you would have the ridiculous situation of a batsman being given out stumped without receiving a ball.

Perhaps you would be good enough to consider the matter and let me know what you think.

The letter I received in reply is reproduced next so that readers can see for themselves the official ruling:

Dear Mr Downes,

Our Administration Manager has passed me you letter regarding the recording of Fair Balls, No Balls and Wide Balls.

The number of balls received by a batsman is of statistical significance with regard to rate of scoring. Awards for such feats as 'the fastest hundred of the season' are based on this rate. A wide ball, by definition, is one from which the striker cannot score. If he 'chases' it and scores from it, it ceases to be a Wide.

It has therefore been decreed that, although a Wide Ball is a 'ball delivered', it is not a 'ball received'. This is the reason for

a) not including the Wides, when totaling up the balls received by Messrs. Stokes and Morris.

b) subtracting the two wides from the 153 balls delivered to check against the total of 151 balls received.

There are those who disagree with the dictum that a Wide is not to count as a ball received, resting their argument, as you do, on the fact that the striker can be given out stumped off a Wide. They are, however, a minority. The dictum is universally applied in the First Class game, and is also very widely applied elsewhere. Everyone who has gained a scoring qualification will know and use it – as indeed will many scorers who are unqualified.

As to the 'ridiculous situation of a batsman being given out stumped without receiving a ball', a batsman can be given out Timed Out, without even reaching the field of play. Moreover, should a new batsman come in as the non-striker, he can be given out. Run Out, Handled the Ball, or Obstructing the Field, his innings consisting of that one delivery, which he did not face.

I hope this is helpful,

Yours sincerely, (etc.)   (Technical Committee Secretary)

FCCQ Question 112:
The lowest innings total by South Africa against England is

The description and reasoning for the method of scoring currently applied is fully understood. However, understanding it as I do, I cannot bring myself to agree with it.

If it is not fair, IT IS NOT CRICKET.

The fault lies in the law that allows a bowler to take a wicket off a Wide Ball which, by definition, is out of reach of the batsman, it is an illegal delivery giving an unfair advantage to the bowler that is NOT CRICKET.

There is a flaw in the acceptance of a No Ball as a "ball received" on the grounds that a batsman can score off a No Ball but not off a Wide. This is not strictly true.

Firstly, in the case of a Wide being called off the same ball as a No Ball, it shall be called a No Ball.

Secondly, an encroachment by the wicket-keeper shall be called a No Ball.

Thirdly, an attempt to run out a striker batsman on his run up by a bowler, successful or not, shall be called a No Ball. In this case the ball is not even delivered, let alone received.

Cricket followers will be aware that a batsman can be out Run Out, Handled Ball or Obstructed the Field following one or more deliveries that he did not face.

FCCQ Question 113:
Which player from either side holds the record for the highest individual score in a series between England and South Africa, and

The "Timed Out" law has a very important part to play and is very effective to the degree that I understand it has never been implemented in the First Class game.

It is essential for a batsman to "receive" a ball in order to be dismissed off it even if it is a Wide. Surely it cannot be said that the batsman did not "receive" it just because he cannot score off it.

Wides count as "Extras" and, as such, are included as runs scored in any partnership that two batsmen may have.

According to the present scoring system, it would be possible for a batsman to come in and the bowler to bowl three Wides in succession, the first one passed the wicket-keeper for four Wides, the second the batsmen ran two Wides and the third one the batsman was Stumped off. A partnership of six runs without either batsman receiving a ball. No wonder it takes a long time to get through the overs these days.

These "Grassroots" observations are offered as constructive criticism in the hope that common sense will prevail and that it must be expected that a batsman is going to be bowled a Wide or two during the course of an Innings and should be registered as such.

There has to be something wrong with the basic rules when "exceptional circumstances" have to be covered as in the following definition from the ACU & S handbook:

FCCQ Question 114.
Name the player not included in the original England touring party, yet took more catches in the 1998-9 9 Ashes series than any other player.

Hit Wicket off a Wide Ball

> Hit Wicket is one of the ways in which the striker can be out if the bowler has bowled a Wide ball. Even though the striker may hit his wicket down before the ball passes the line of the stumps, both the penalty for the Wide ball and the dismissal will stand except in two special situations which are most unlikely to occur. If the striker hits his wicket before the ball is delivered, on appeal, and providing the ball is delivered, the striker will be given out at the moment of delivery and any subsequent action is irrelevant. The other exceptional circumstance is when, at the end of a match, nine wickets are down and one run is needed to win. In this case it has been decided that the Hit Wicket dismissal counts and the match is at an end; the penalty for the Wide is not awarded.

Imagine the mayhem if a player has been out stumped or hit wicket to a last ball wide in the recent tied World Cup semi-final. How many of the fifteen personnel on the field of play would have known the ruling, and not forgetting the one with the TV Monitor.

No, I think it would be far better and certainly fairer that it were not possible for a bowler to take a wicket off a wide and the only reason for loss of wickets to be as defined for a no ball.

FCCQ Question 115:
Hedley Verity holds the record for the best bowling return in First Class Cricket. How may runs did he concede in taking?

WORLD CUP CRICKET

That the World Cup 1999 was a success, there is some doubt. That it could have been a great success, there is no doubt.

The timing of the event I do not question, as who knows when the sun will shine or the rain will fall in a British summer? To have only one match when there was no result was a remarkable achievement.

In my opinion, the complete format was all wrong! It would have been much better to have played 66 matches where every team played one another, where all 6 matches were played on the same day. This would have taken no longer than the system used in 1999.

This would, obviously, have been a much fairer competition. There are other advantages. For example, Scotland did not get to play Kenya and neither side won a game – such a game would have been watched with great anticipation in both countries.

With six games being played simultaneously, the matches could have been shared by the rival television companies and transmitted to the participating countries, thus generating more revenue.
No team would be given any advantage over any other as all would have the same number of rest days between matches.

Where the teams finish level on points, I do not believe that the run rate is the fairest criterion to decide the issue as this method gives a distinct advantage to the side batting second.

FCCQ Question 116:
Name the most economical bowler in the 1999 World Cup.

GROUP A FINAL STANDINGS
(revised to include average runs per wicket differentials instead of run rate)

The method I would advocate is on averages of runs per wicket as indicated in the following table. The taking and saving of wickets plays a far more significant role.

For Runs-for-wkts-ave = ave	against runs-for-wkts = ave
S Africa 1016 – 35 = 29.02	851 – 41 + 20.75 = + 8.26
India 1392 – 31 = 44.90	1154 – 39 + 29.58 = + 15.32
Zimbabwe 1080 – 37 = 29.18	1029 – 36 = 29.18 = +0.59
England 851 – 26 = 32.75	1031 – 43 = 23.97 = + 8.76
Sri Lanka 1003 – 44 = 22.79	1106 – 32 = 34.56 = –1.51
Kenya 1049 – 40 = 26.22	1192 – 19 = 62.73 = –36.50

Before starting this exercise, I had no idea how it would work out. However, it is interesting to note that England would have leapfrogged over Zimbabwe and qualified for the final stages of the tournament.

In Group B, the differentials were as follows:

New Zealand	+16.41
Australia	+10.71
West Indies	+8.63
Pakistan	+6.93
Scotland	–7.10
Bangladesh	–17.95

In this table, the only change would have been that Scotland would change places with Bangladesh.

FCCQ Question 117:
Name the bowler with the best strike rate in the 1999 World Cup

The most exciting game of the World Cup without question was the semi-final that resulted in a tie.

Once again, I believe the rules were wrong in that the winners should have been decided on the run rate of the previous matches. This must have been even harder for South Africa to accept when you consider that they won one more match than Australia in reaching the final.

As two days were allocated for the game in case of adverse weather conditions, why was there not a replay on the second day – a guaranteed full house and a lot more revenue?

If an instant result is required when even the Duckworthf/Lewis method fails to produce one, I have a solution.

Play to the gallery. First, one side bowls an over at an unmanned wicket. This would produce anything from 0 to 6 wickets, it may also produce extras in the way of No balls or Wides.

Following this, the batsmen would be introduced to have six free hits the number of batsmen used would depend on the number of wickets taken in the previous over at the unguarded wicket.

There would need to be batsmen at the non-strikers end as runs, other than boundaries, would have to be run and it would be possible to lose another wicket, run out. No fielding restrictions of any description. How's that for instant cricket?

FCCQ Question 118:
Name the batsman to score the most runs in the 1999 World Cup.

BACK TO GRASSROOTS

As we approach the twenty first century, I am pleased to confirm that grassroots cricket is still fun as will be indicated in this report that I did after having the pleasure of watching the last league game of the season between Conwy and Shotton in the third division of the Readers Romida North Wales League in which two of my grandsons were playing.

The match finished just after six o' clock, but the drama spilt over into the clubhouse and two hours later to the Rhos Fynnoch Tavern where the club secretary, Dick Weed, took various phone calls to clarify the situation.

It had been a good game of cricket and Conwy first team had managed to do something that had thwarted them twice before this season when in winning positions. Not only had they won, but they had beaten the weather as rain followed them off the field.

Eric Shilicock had done what every good captain should do and won the toss, promptly asking Shotton to bat. After a slow start, wickets gradually started to fall, five to Paul Williams, four to Dave Wilkinson and one to Nick Davis helped by two smart catches behind the stumps by Mike Steen the visitors were all out for 122 after being 80 for 8 when rain caused a brief stoppage.

The bowlers, backed by some good ground fielding in spite of the dead grass cuttings lying in the outfield, had done a good job.

FCCQ Question 119:
In what year was the first Test Match played at Lords?

The skipper then made his second major decision and sent in Ian Macdonald to open the innings with the redoubtable Graham Fraser. It was not long before the short leg removed his protective headgear and retreated fifteen yards into the deep

Fifty runs were added without loss, the century partnership. On course for maximum points so far and assured promotion, six runs needed for victory and six for Ian's century. Alas he was out caught at square leg and a vital point had been dropped. Time was no problem as twenty-two overs still remained in which to score six precious runs. Two maiden overs were bowled and the rain clouds gathered. Then three Wides were bowled as the bowlers tried a defensive leg side theory.

The wind started to blow and the temperature began to fall rapidly. Suddenly Steven Lloyd, batting at number three, made an off drive for two to level the scores. The next ball, a late cut for that all important single. Graham Frazer had carried has bat once again for 18 hard earned runs.

However, there is no doubt that Ian Macdonald's 94, which included four sixes, was the best innings of the season and earned Conwy a 9 point to 1 point win.

At the beginning of the game, Castel Alun were top of the table with 123 points, Conwy second with 123 points and Pwllheli third, also with 123 points. Bala were fourth with 121 points. So before the last round of matches, any two of four clubs could be promoted.

FCCQ Question 120:
In what year did Easter Coaching Classes start at Lords?

So the drama that followed Conwy's thrilling win meant that they would at least finish third but the other two clubs could, mathematically, still score more than Conwy's revised total of 132 points.

As tension mounted and the bar stocks fell, news filtered through that the rain had beaten the unfortunate Castel Alun.

Promotion had been achieved, but who were the champions? News came through that Pwllheli were still playing but the score was not known.

Then it was revealed that that Pwllheli had won. But by what margin? How many? Eight points to two.

Altogether Conwy – "WE ARE THE CHAMPIONS"

It must be remembered that the result of one game does not win the league title, and that there have been various heroes during the season in this that has a good mixture of experience and youth, but most of all, team spirit.

This team spirit was exemplified on Saturday by the Chairman, veteran Alan Lavery, who enthusiastically substituted for the youngest member of the side 14 year old Adam Shillcock who was injured, no doubt as a result of playing a soccer match in the morning. The current eleven should, however, avoid complacency as there are some mature sixteen year olds in the second team that will be pressing for the opportunity to do battle with Liandudno, Aberegele and Llanwrst next year.

FCCQ Question 121:
If a no-ball evades the batsman and wicket keeper and strikes a helmet on the ground behind the keeper, what would be entered in the score book?

That grassroots cricket is still fun and that grassroots cricketers still have a sense of humour is endorsed by this incident that my wife and I witnessed.

As Sports development officer, our one son-in-law David, always sets a fine example by carrying a sports medical kit in his car and has had cause to use it on a number of occasions whilst watching Conwy Cricket Club.A game at Bethesda had been in progress over an hour when David arrived at the ground when, within seconds, one of the players crashed into a concrete block in front of the scoreboard in attempting to field a ball.

It was obvious that the fielder had injured himself and in double quick time David was administering first aid. As the Conwy fielders gathered round' the vice captain, Jamie Wilkinson, came running over saying "It's fantastic. Blooming marvellous how he appears at the crucial moment when there's a crisis, just like Kate Adie."

FCCQ Question 122:
If the ball deflected off the wicket keepers pads to first slip, would it be possible for that player to make a stumping?

FIRST CLASS CRICKET QUIZ ANSWERS

1. With Sheep
2. Dorset Fields
3. The Regents Canal
4. 1814
5. William Gilbert
6. Old Father Time Weather Vane
7. 1870
8. Albert Trott
9. England by 5 Wickets
10. Only player to score Test Century on Test debut at Lords
11. 5
12. First and Tenth
13. TilakRaj
14. 12
15. 80
16. Wilfred Rhodes
17. DJGSales
18. AEFagg
19. WHPonsford
20. India
21. Throwing (bowling round arm)
22. Shares eighth wicket record of 124 with E.H. Hendren
23. 2000 Test Runs and 200 Test Wickets
24. Yes, if the batsman is attempting to avoid being hit
25. Any appeal would be given Not Out
26. 5.5 oz and 5.75 oz
27. 5 feet, being a total of 10 feet in width
28. 2, Hit Wicket and Stumped
29. Penalty extra for bowling Wide still stands
30. 5, Hit Wicket, Stumped, Run Out, Handled Ball, Obstruction
31. Steve Buckner

32. Nigel Plews
33. 4, Balderston, Hampshire, Holder and Willey
34. 66
35. 1972
36. Leicestershire
37. 1963
38. Sussex
39. SFBarnes49
40. WRHammond 905
41. SMGavaskar34
42. HTrumble
43. Lancashire
44. Leicestershire
45. 181 mins
46. 552
47. 81 Turner and East
48. W Gunn and J.R. Gunn
49. GHick
50. W.G. Grace
51. 22
52. G.H.Hurst
53. C.L. Townsend
54. WHBraine
55. L.Hutton
56. GBoycott
57. Northamptonshire, 12
58. Yorkshire, 887
59. C.B. Fry
60. F. E. Wooley
61. W.R. Hammond,36
62. D. V. Wright, 7
63. W. R. Hammond, 10
64. L. E. G. Aimes, 128
65. G. Hick and T. Moody

66. G. Hick

67. L. Hutton, 1294

68. Oand0

69. G. Lloyd

70. G. Lloyd

71. G. Lloyd

72. S. James

73. G. Hick

74. A. M. Smith, 83—highest wicket taker 1997

75. S. A. Marsh

76. T. R. Ward

77. 3

78. 5, V. J. Marks

79. 80*, Bairstow and Johnston

80. 38 and *4.5* inches respectively

81. No

82. Yes

83. S. P.James

84. G. A. Hick_303*

85. 12

86. D. Ripley

87. D. CNash

88. 20

89. 2, Thorpe and Crawley

90. England 18, Australia 14

91. England 4, Australia 8

92. England 3, Australia 7

93. England *5,* Australia 6

94. England 0, Australia 1

95. 1 for England (G. P. Thorpe), 2 for Australia (Reifell and Elliott)

96. Double of 100 wickets and 1000 Runs in Tests

97. A.A. Donald

98. I. P. Tuffnell

99   198, G. Gooch
100 10.75
101 E. E. Hemmings
102 I. V. A. Richards
103 No
104 The Batsman who hit the ball
105 Yes, if it has been made prior to the first ball of the next over and
        time has not been called.
106 Cancel his decision
107 Infringement by Wicket keeper
108 Re-erect one of the stumps
109 Only one run deducted
110 G. M. Griffin
111 A. A. Donald
112 30
113 E. A. B. Rowan, 236
114 G. Hick
115 10
116 C. A. Walsh – West Indies
117 J. A. R. Blain – Scotland
118 R. S. Dravid – India
119 1884
120 1902
121 6 No balls
122 No, the Batsman would be Run Out. Only the Wicket keeper can
make a Stumping

LIILLESHALL TRIP NAMES

1 Best	38 Cook	75 Darling
2 How	39 Lamb	76 lane
3 Bus)s)	40 Butcher	77 bailey
4 Chappel	41 Close 7	8 Brook
5 Compton	42 Car)r)	79 Street
6 Wait(e)	43 Butcher	80 Long
7 Gray	44 Coney	81 Cake
8 House	45 Agnew	82 Wild
9 Hill	46 Knight	83 Amiss
10 Fry	47 Atherton	84 Grace
11Key	48 Stewart	85 Mailey
12 Lock	49 Hussain	86 Caesar
13 Old	50 Crawley	87 King
14 Wooler	51 But(t)	88 Bedser
15 Li(le)y	52 Thorpe	89Crapp
16 Barber	53 Cork	90 Virgin
17 Long	54 Croft	91 Laker
18 Snow	55 Gough	92 Newport
19 Conway	56 Caddick	93 Nash
20 Douglas	57 Tufnell	94 Sobers
21 Pick	58 Russell	95 Shastri
22 Bill	59 But(t)	96 Wardle
23 Mold	60 Knott	97 Berry
24 Andrew	61 Bracewell	98 Underwood
25 Flint	62 Hadlee	99 East
26 Shrewsbury	63 Read	100 Childs
27 Contractor	64 Gower	101 Edmunds
28 Tiler	65 Benuad	102 Lee
29 Wall	66 Boycott	103 Young
30 Grout	67 May	104 White
31 Carpenter	68 Daft	105 Slade
32 Bannister	69 Week(e)s	106 Gifford
33 Hall	70 Holding	107 Botham
34 Brain	71 Loader	
35 Flowers	72 Nurse	
36 Valentine	73 Ward	
37 Taylor	74 Hick	

The batsman who hit six consecutive sixes in England was MIKE PROCTOR. The bowler was DENIS BREAKWELL who played for Hobsons at Worfield with his father, Jack, who, at the time, also played for Dudley in the Birmingham League.

* * * * *

For answers to the two questions on the book cover, ask your club umpire.

No, on second thoughts, refer to the official textbook of the Association of Cricket Umpires and Scorers.

Tom Smith's *Cricket Umpiring and Scoring*.

Every club should have a copy.

FAMILY ANSWERS

1

	FATHERS	SONS
a	Alan Butcher	Mark & Gary
b	Cohn Cowdrey	Graham
c	Ron Headley	Dean
d	David Lloyd	Graham
e	Barry Wood	Nathan
f	David Steel	Mark
g	Bruce Cairns	Christopher
h	Bob Cottam	Andrew
i	Alan Knott	James
j	Micky Stewart	Alec
h	Mike Smith	Neil

2

a Robin and Philip Weston
b Darren and Martin Bicknell
c Adam and Ben Hollioake
d Keith and Mark Newell
e Mark and Gary Butcher
f Alex and Graham Swann

3 Surrey
4 Colin and Chris Cowdrey
5 George, Ron and Dean Headley
6 John Steel
7 Alan Ealham
8 Bill Blenkiron and Doug Slade

ABC ANSWERS

1.	Alderman	2.	Bradman	3.	Chapman
4.	Dowman	5.	Freeman	6.	Jackman
7.	Mankad	8.	O'Gorman	9.	Swetman

Sir Alex Douglas Home is quoted as saying, "if there be cricket in

heaven, let there also be rain." This prompted my

FINAL SELECTION

If there be cricket in heaven,
oh, Lord, let me be in the eleven.
For I know it would need an act of God
to be named in such an illustrious squad
Cricket in heaven would be bliss
not a single days play would we miss.
Rain or bad light would never stop play.
The sun would shine to the end of the day.
The rain would fall at night
the days would be sunny and bright.
In the gentle warmth of the sun
Cricket would certainly be fun.
Batsman when out would never linger
and wait for an umpire to raise his finger.
If there was a chance ball had hit ground
there would be no appeal, no not a sound.
So pick a squad if you dare.
First criteria, that they all play fair.
Not for glory, but the love of the game.
If that's the case, then let's have his name.
There are ten ways to be out, as given to Moses.
So think again of the problem that poses.
The laws are harder, I think you'll agree,
the chance of selection looks slim to me